BBQ POCKET GUIDE

By Remus Powers, Ph.B.

Pig Out Publications, Inc.
Kansas City, Missouri

Copyright © 1992 by Pig Out Publications, Inc.

All rights reserved. No part of this book may be reproduced or transmitted in any form or by any means, electronic or mechanical, including photocopying, recording, or by any information storage and retrieval system, without prior written permission from Pig Out Publications, Inc.

The cartoon "Did You Bring Sauce?", copyright © 1982 by Lee Judge, originally appeared in the *Kansas City Times*. Reproduced by permission.

ISBN 0-925175-20-X

Printed in the United States of America

Please send comments and suggestions for future editions to:
    Remus Powers, Ph.B.
    c/o Pig Out Publications, Inc.
    11514 Hickman Mills Rd.
    Kansas City, MO 64134

For Arthur Bryant

Rest in Peace

CONTENTS

ACKNOWLEDGMENTS 7

A CONSUMER'S GUIDE TO SWINE DINING ON THE URBAN PRAIRIE 10

GLOSSARY 17

BARBECUE LOCATOR MAP 19

KANSAS CITY 'QUE FROM ALLEN'S TO ZARDA
    Allen's Bar-B-Que 25
    B.B.'s Lawn Side Bar-B-Q 27
    The Big Q Barbecue 28
    Boardroom Bar-B-Q 29
    Bodee's Bar-B-Que 31
    Boyds 'n Son Bar-B-Q 33
    Arthur Bryant's Barbecue 35
    CJ's Bar-B-Que 36
    Coyote Grill 38
    Jake Edwards Bar-B-Que 39
    Farmer's B-B-Q 41
    Gates & Sons Bar-B-Q 42
    Grand Emporium Saloon 44
    Guy & Mae's Tavern 46
    Hayward's Pit Bar-B-Que 47
    Heartland Bar-B-Que 49
    Hillsdale Bank Bar-B-Q 51
    Houston's 53
    Jimmy's Jigger 55
    Johnny's Hickory House Bar-B-Q 56

K.C. Masterpiece Barbecue & Grill 58
Keegan's Bar-B-Q 60
Knight's Barbecue 61
Lil' Jake's Eat It & Beat It 63
Longbranch Saloon 64
Mark & Jerry's Bar-B-Que Buffet 65
Marty's Bar-B-Q 66
Original Smoke Bar-B-Que 68
O'Toole and Sons Ribs 70
Porky's Pit Bar-B-Q 71
Earl Quick's Bar-B-Q 72
Ribs 'n Stuff 74
Ricky's Pit Bar-B-Que 76
Rosedale Barbeque 77
Rouse's Bar-B-Que 78
Rustler's Hickory Pit Bar-B-Q 80
Santa Fe Trail Bar-B-Q 81
7th Street Bar-B-Q 83
Smoke Stack Bar-B-Q of Martin City 84
Smokin' Joe's BBQ 86
Snead's Bar-B-Q 88
Werner's Specialty Foods 89
Westport Bar-B-Que 91
Winslow's City Market Smokehouse 93
Wyandot Bar-B-Q 94
Zarda Bar-B-Q 95

KANSAS CITY BARBECUE GIFTS AND PRODUCTS 97

KANSAS CITY AREA BARBECUE COOKING CONTESTS 106

BARBECUE BUCKS 111

ACKNOWLEDGMENTS

The Hutanga people who lived and hunted in what's now the Kansas City metropolitan area engaged in "vision quests." Participants journeyed alone to an isolated piece of wilderness for several days of fasting and self-inflicted pain, which brought on the sought-after visions.

A good friend once told me "Opposites are the same." She was talking about people in relationships, but I've found that the principle can also apply to vision quests. My Barbecue Vision Quest in the preparation of this book has been the opposite of solitude, fasting, and self-inflicted pain. Nevertheless, the discipline of research and writing has rewarded me with knowledge and ideas unique to this particular journey. I haven't had visions, but I've sharpened my understanding of the mythological and cultural role barbecue plays in Kansas City and in our society. That's another subject, another book. I've also met some good people and eaten some excellent barbecue. I do hope some wisdom, vision, and humor have visited this pocket guide as a result.

Scores of friends, acquaintances, colleagues, and role models have contributed time, opinions, ideas, information, inspiration, and encouragement. Without them this book would have remained an idea instead of a tangible product.

First, I am grateful to my immediate family, Gretchen, Sarah, and Lee, for patience, encouragement, and understanding when I made working on this book a priority over bird watching, strolling and visiting in Loose Park, or taking a day trip. They also were willing and helpful partners in some of the research.

Karen Adler persuaded me to do this book in a discussion over a plate of ribs, beef, and sausage at Rouse's. Despite the stress of deadlines and juggling of priorities, it has been a fun book to write. Karen and her partner in the Pig Out Publications venture, Carolyn Wells, Ph.B., have provided essential encouragement and support. Jane Guthrie did a superb job of editing this volume.

John Bowes of Topeka and Glenna Stites of Johnson County Community College were invaluable in getting me to a functional level of Wordperfect 5.1 proficiency. John also was an able proofreader and made several suggestions that became part of this book.

Stuart Hall, Inc. of Kansas City still makes the Big Chief tablets I used for drafting the manuscript and making research notes. Big Chief serves as my writing muse.

Walt Bodine's example of saying what you like about a place and not mentioning what you don't like is a guiding principle here. When there's a new rib joint in town, Walt is one of the first to find it. His Kansas City rib reports appear regularly on KMBC Channel 9 News. Several ribs reviewed in this book owe to my learning about them through Walt's reporting.

WDAF 61 Country's early morning deejay David Lawrence puts a smile on my face and a positive attitude in my brain each weekday morning on the way to work. Sky Spy Christy Russell, Ag Reporter Mark Oppold, and wordsmith meteorologist Elliott Abrams are the perfect complement to David's style. Kansas City barbecue is a frequent topic on 61 Country.

Lee Judge, the *Kansas City Star*'s irreverent political cartoonist, did the Remus Powers, Ph.B. caricature used in this book. Remus as portrayed by Judge has helped spread a lot of good humor throughout the national barbecue network. Thank you, Lee, and thanks also for permission to use your classic, "Did You Bring Sauce?"

I've dined with a lot of people and have asked for many opinions in an effort to get beyond my own likes and dislikes when evaluating K.C. barbecue restaurants. Thanks sincerely to Paul Kirk, C.W.C./Ph.B., Susan and Steven Hill, Gloria Walker, Mike McKenzie, Laura Bostrom, Donna Bodinson, Ann Davis, Steve Parman, Kayla Musick, Mary Lou Hester, Bill McGuff, Joanne Hurst, Alice Knatt, Richard Wagner, Don Lambert, John Kelly, Richard Hernandez, Clarence Rhambo, Tom Morrow, Paul Showalter, Kevin Siek, Sharon Joseph, Steve and Janice Katz, Lou and Joan Rardin, Jim and Peg Davidson, Dick and Linda Barrett, Marceline Taylor, Dick Henderson, Dorothy Billingsley, Clyde Calhoun, Jr., Barbara Hickingbotham, Jim Mackie, Linda Ray, Rose Kemp, Leann Ritter, Grace Kilbane, Herman Wallace, Jim Gohlston, Greg Wilder, and Robert Rios, to name a few.

Finally, thanks and applause to Kansas City's many

pitmasters and to the members of the Kansas City Barbeque Society.

If your favorite K.C. barbecue restaurant isn't in here, be assured that omissions owe to time and space, and do not reflect on the quality of the establishments not reviewed. Watch for them in future editions.

A CONSUMER'S GUIDE TO SWINE DINING ON THE URBAN PRAIRIE

> *Kansas City–Barbecue Central: This is it: Ground Zero, America's premier melting pot of smoke and sauce, the headquarters of hickory, Cow Town Central, the Capital of Que. Where else but in Kansas City could you have the most famous barbecue joint in the world—and it's not even the best in town? Where else could you find hot sauce in the airport gift shop?*
>
> *Other cities can claim to be the Barbecue Center of the Universe. But no place puts it all together like K.C., a one-city crash course in American barbecue. Choosing one joint in Kansas City as the "best" is as pointless an exercise as looking down a row of Rockettes and worrying about who has the best knee dimples. The thing about Kansas City is that you don't have to choose: It's all there for the sampling. Lots of places have their strong points, and it's hard to find a loser.*

Vince Staten and Greg Johnson, *Real Barbecue*
(New York: Harper & Row Publishers, 1988)

This book features a lion's share of Kansas City metropolitan area barbecue restaurants, plus some outside the city, beyond suburbia. We've included a few spots that don't specialize in barbecue, and there's a place or two that call some of their food "barbecue," but it qualifies only under the most liberal of definitions.

This is *not* the local restaurant guidebook that Jinx and Jefferson Morgan of *Bon Appetit* magazine warned you about. "Watch out," they said, "for those that are simply vehicles for advertising in which an ad guarantees a favorable listing." This book is an ad for the richness of Kansas City barbecue. The emphasis is on the positive. Our aim is to tell you what we think you'll like about each restaurant. There's no rating system of stars, oinks, or other symbols.

There are some ads in the form of "barbecue bucks" at the back of the book, but buying a buck wasn't a requirement for being mentioned here. Our primary purpose is to introduce Kansas City visitors and residents to some of the best barbecue restaurants in town.

No matter who you are and where you come from, you have roots in Kansas City. Here on the urban prairie, traders, speculators, farmers, miners, educators, politicians, and all manner of other persons have spent time on their way to seek a fortune or a better life. Your great-great grandfather or grandmother, your father, mother, brother, sister, aunt, uncle, or cousin—more than one of them has stopped in Kansas City over the last 200 years or so. So you have roots here. Welcome home.

Now that your Kansas City heritage is understood, how about barbecue? How and why has Kansas City become so famous worldwide for a method of cooking born in East Africa over a million years ago?

Kansas City BBQ History

The definitive history of Kansas City barbecue is yet to be written. Neal Willis, Ph.D., a professor of psychology at the University of Missouri–Kansas City, is working on it. Until Neal's research is finished and his book is published, we're left with a sketchy perception, peopled by some of the big names in Kansas City's recent past. Their success with ribs and brisket has made Kansas City famous for barbecue. Henry Perry, Charlie Bryant, Arthur Bryant, George Gates, Ollie Gates, Otis Boyd, and Anthony Rieke represent the legacy of Kansas City barbecue as we know it today, going back only as late as the 1920s, when barbecue and jazz jammin' sessions thrived in this town.

The abundant proximity of hickory, oak, and stockyards meat, combined with pitmaster skills brought here by a culturally diverse group of immigrants, is the theme of modern Kansas City barbecue history. Literally hundreds of barbecue businesses have come and gone in Kansas City in less than 80 years. A few restaurants, such as Gates, Bryant's, and Rosedale, have survived the longest in today's competitive Kansas City barbecue market. In the dynamic milieu of Kansas City BBQ, one constant has endured: the public's appetite for Kansas City–style meats from the pit.

Que-linary Advice for Greasehouse Adventurers

A Big Mistake in matters of taste is deference to so-called "experts." When barbecue visits your palate, let there be no question as to who is the expert. You are it. Sometimes you'll discover excellent barbecue that has been berated by other experts. Sometimes you'll agree with them. *Just be true to your own taste.*

Remember at all times and in all greasehouses: There is no universal standard for excellence. Barbecue experts use three que-linary guidelines in evaluating barbecue, and at least seven for discovering the most likely places to find good barbecue.

I. Judging the Barbecue on Your Plate

Experts evaluate appearance, tenderness, and taste. Kansas City Barbeque Society president Gary Wells calls this "the AT&T of judging barbecue."

A. Appearance

Appearance is evaluated subjectively and objectively. Subjective standards vary by individual and by culture; smoke rings and presentation are the two most important objective standards.

1. *Smoke ring:* A red smoke ring offers visible proof that the meat has been smoked. The smoke ring will show on the outside edge of ribs, beef brisket, and pork shoulder. Sometimes ribs will be completely red from smoke. The smoke ring will appear next to the bone in poultry. Don't mistake smoked poultry for raw poultry.

Due to differences in holding methods and the passage of time from the pit to the plate, some commercial barbecue doesn't show a smoke ring. This costs precious points at barbecue cooking contests, but it isn't important to most restaurant customers. If you can't see the evidence of smoke, you should still be able to taste it. If you don't see smoke rings and/or don't taste smoke, you aren't eating barbecue.

2. *Presentation:* What you see on the plate sends a message to your palate. When food looks and smells good, we think it will taste good. Woe to the pitmaster who disappoints us.

Presentation begins with the outside appearance of the restaurant and ends as you walk out the door and leave the premises. Most of what happens to you from the beginning to the end of your dining experience—the ambience and the eating—is part of the restaurant's presentation. When the ribber eats the rib, and the rib is good, it transforms what was first seen as a mere greasehouse into what is now seen as a RIB PALACE.

There are no universal standards for the presentation of barbecued food. Barbecue may be served on fine china, sterling silver, crystal, glass, stoneware, plastic, foam, foil, butcher paper, or other forms of plates and platters. Pitmasters who care about their product will show care and pride in the arrangement of the food on whatever the serving surface. Consistency is also important. You will come to expect a certain signature style of presentation at each restaurant.

Kansas City barbecue restaurant decor ranges from simple to elegant. Some resemble fast feeders. Some are country-western style. Some are bars—jazz bars, blues bars, neighborhood bars. Some are fancy and some are just plain greasehouses. There is almost as much variety in K.C. barbecue restaurant decor as there is in the variety of barbecue available.

B. Tenderness

Tender barbecue is easy to chew and swallow. It needn't be so tender that it falls off the bone. My personal preference is crisp on the outside and tender on the inside.

C. Taste

Taste is the single most important standard for judging barbecue. It also enjoys the least consensus. This is where you must listen to your own taste buds.

In general, good barbecue tastes smoky, not bitter or bland. It has enough grease to flavor the meat but not define it. The meat is hot. It tastes rich, not anemic. It is packed with a symphony of flavors that can only be produced with a pit, fire, smoke, secret seasonings, and the care and attention of a skilled pitmaster.

Sauce should only be desirable, not necessary. And it should be desired only if it truly complements the flavor of the meat instead of overpowering it. If the meat can't stand alone on good flavor, leave it alone.

Grease can detract from or enhance taste. One of the virtues of good barbecue is that the slow cooking process allows much of the grease to escape, leaving the heavenly essence of tender, smoked meat. The remainder enhances the flavor and tenderness of the meat.

II. Finding a Good Greasehouse

Some of the signals I've learned for finding a good greasehouse were taught to me by the Coronado of American Barbecue, Vince Staten. Vince travels across the U.S.A. in a never-ending search for Greasehouse Gold. He described some of his discoveries with coauthor and Doctor of Barbecue Philosophy in his own right, Greg Johnson, in one of the best barbecue books of the century, *Real Barbecue*.

These signals aren't 100% reliable 100% of the time. Serendipity can always pop up when you least expect it. But if you use these signals and the que-linary guidelines and trust yourself, you won't go home hungry and disappointed.

Here's what Vince taught me, along with some of my own learnings:

A. Name

A good greasehouse will bear the name of its owner. No self-respecting Bubba, Bob, or Johnny would put his own name and reputation on a place that sells bad barbecue.

B. Woodpile

If you don't see a woodpile outside, think twice about going inside. If the woodpile is neatly stacked, like it's just for show, think twice again. Find out if the wood is actually used for the barbecue. The wood should be hickory, oak, pecan, or other hardwoods or fruitwoods. Under all circumstances avoid places cluttered with scraps from local tree-trimming services. Elm, cottonwood, locust, and maple don't smoke with a Kansas City accent.

C. Vehicles

A combo of pickup trucks, vans, Volvos, BMWs, Porsches, Chevrolets, Fords, Colts, Cadillacs, Continentals, and Toyotas is a good sign. When lawyers, professors, CPAs, bureaucrats, politicians, and rednecks think it's good barbecue, you're probably going to think so, too.

D. Windows

Don't trust clean windows. Pit time, not spit shine, is what's important in a greasehouse. The greasehouse is one place where you want to see through a glass darkly.

E. Signs
Greasehouse signs should advertise barbecue—not hot dogs, hamburgers, or tacos. If the pitmaster isn't making a living on the quality of the barbecue, it doesn't speak well for the place. A "Chili" sign, though, is O.K.; it's a hospitable concession to visiting Texans and Seattlelites.

F. Flies
If you don't see any flies near the premises, the flies may know something that you should know.

G. Friendly service
In the best greasehouses you'll feel welcome the moment you step inside. If a place has a bad attitude but good barbecue, get carryout. If a place has a good attitude and good barbecue, dine in and come back often.

Swine Dining Etiquette

Barbecue should be eaten from hand to mouth, just as our ancestors ate it thousands of years ago. It is impossible to eat this way without getting grease and sauce on your hands and face, but don't worry about it. It's O.K. to get messy.

Swine dining style—or how you pick up the meat and eat and chew—is a matter of personal preference. Your style does make a statement about who you are or how you wish to be seen. There are left-handed, right-handed, and both-handed styles. Rib eaters may go from left to right, right to left, or start in the middle and go right or left. You may eat with gusto or with reserve.

Your finished rib bones also make a statement. A clean bone, says Paul Kirk, C.W.C./Ph.B. and KC Baron of Barbecue, is a sign of a true ribber.

Sandwiches are a modern twist to the presentation of barbecue. Putting the meat between bread slices is popular but unnecessary. In Kansas City the most common bread used for barbecue sandwiches is the cheap white kind, preferred because the flavor doesn't get in the way of the meat. It's also good for soaking up sauce and grease.

Finally, avoid getting so absorbed in style that you don't enjoy the food. The greasehouse is a pre-etiquette environment where you should feel free to be yourself and indulge in the food as our ancestors did.

Call Ahead

Before adventuring to any Kansas City barbecue restaurant, it's a good idea to call ahead, to be sure they're open when you plan to arrive. And ask for directions on how to get there, regardless of your gender.

Since accessibility for people with disabilities isn't coded in the book, please ask about it if you or anyone in your party uses a wheelchair or has other special needs. Compliance with architectural standards established in the Americans with Disabilities Act is, thankfully, making swine dining possible for everyone.

Finally, if you're sensitive to second-hand tobacco smoke, ask about the smoking policy of the restaurant and about the quality of the ventiliation system in the dining areas.

Autograph It

Enhance the historical and personal value of this book by collecting autographs of K.C. pitmasters and staffers who give you a memorable swine-dining experience.

Make your own notes in the margins, indicating when you visited the restaurant and what you liked/didn't like about it. Ask your dining companions to autograph it, too.

GLOSSARY

Baby back ribs Short, curved ribs from a pig's back; usually less meaty than spareribs. Commonly served in St. Louis and mid-South cities such as Memphis, but available in some K.C. restaurants.

Barbecue According to the U.S. Government, "Barbecued meats . . . shall be cooked by the direct action of dry heat resulting from the burning of hard wood or the hot coals therefrom for a sufficient period to assume the usual characteristics of a barbecued article, which include formation of a brown crust on the surface and the rendering of surface fat. The product may be basted with a sauce during the cooking process. The weight of barbecued meat shall not exceed 70 percent of the weight of the fresh uncooked meat" (9 CFR, Part 319, Subpart C, Section 319.80, revised as of January 1, 1985). Meat baked in a gas or electric oven and seasoned with barbecue sauce may taste good, but it isn't real barbecue.

Brisket The tough breast muscle from cattle.

Burnt ends The crispy crusted meat from a barbecue beef brisket. Often, due to scarce supply, what is offered as "burnt ends" is simply chunks of beef with now and then a crispy piece, smothered in sauce. When Arthur Bryant was alive, burnt ends were free to anyone who wanted to reach in and grab some on the way through the line. With his passing went the best burnt ends ever produced on the planet.

Finishing sauce A seasoned liquid applied to meat at the last 20 to 30 minutes of cooking. It is often served atop meat unless requested on the side (a recommended practice until you decide if you like the sauce).

Gimme cap A one-size-fits-all duck-billed cap worn by baseball players, farmers, barbecuers, Indianapolis 500 spectators, and other diverse elements of our society. Most advertise a product; when first introduced as a walking ad form, eager consumers asked their implements dealer to please "gimme."

Grilling A method of cooking meat directly over hot coals or flames. Not to be confused with barbecue.

Hogmatism A condition of narrow-mindedness and imagined que-linary infallibility; related to dogmatism. Typical symptoms are remarks such as "If you think this is good barbecue, you don't know smoke from shinola!"

Long end The end of a rib slab with the longest, but less meaty, ribs (usually six ribs).

Marinade A liquid or dry seasoning mix applied to meat several hours before cooking that sometimes includes tenderizing agents.

Mopping sauce/baste A seasoned liquid applied to meat during the cooking process; usually heavy on vinegar and light on sugars or catsup to allow penetration and avoid burning or caramelizing.

Pitmaster One who tends the pit with expertise. He or she has mastered the barbecue method of cooking and may be either a professional or an amateur.

Redneck A person who spends enough time in the sun to get sunburn on the back of the neck and is intolerant of views not held by him or her; see "hogmatism."

Rib tips Technically, the ends trimmed off rib slabs; in practice, that plus other rib trimmings. More grease and gristle, but great taste.

Short end The end of a rib slab with the short, meaty bones (usually seven ribs).

Rub A mixture of dry herbs, spices, and other seasonings rubbed on meat to enhance its flavor; may be added before, during, or after cooking. Sometimes called "rib rub."

Spare ribs Pork rib slabs, cut from behind the shoulder of the hog.

"Struttin' with Some Barbecue" A popular song recorded by Louis Armstrong in 1927; adapted by Gates and Sons as a corporate slogan.

BARBECUE LOCATOR MAP

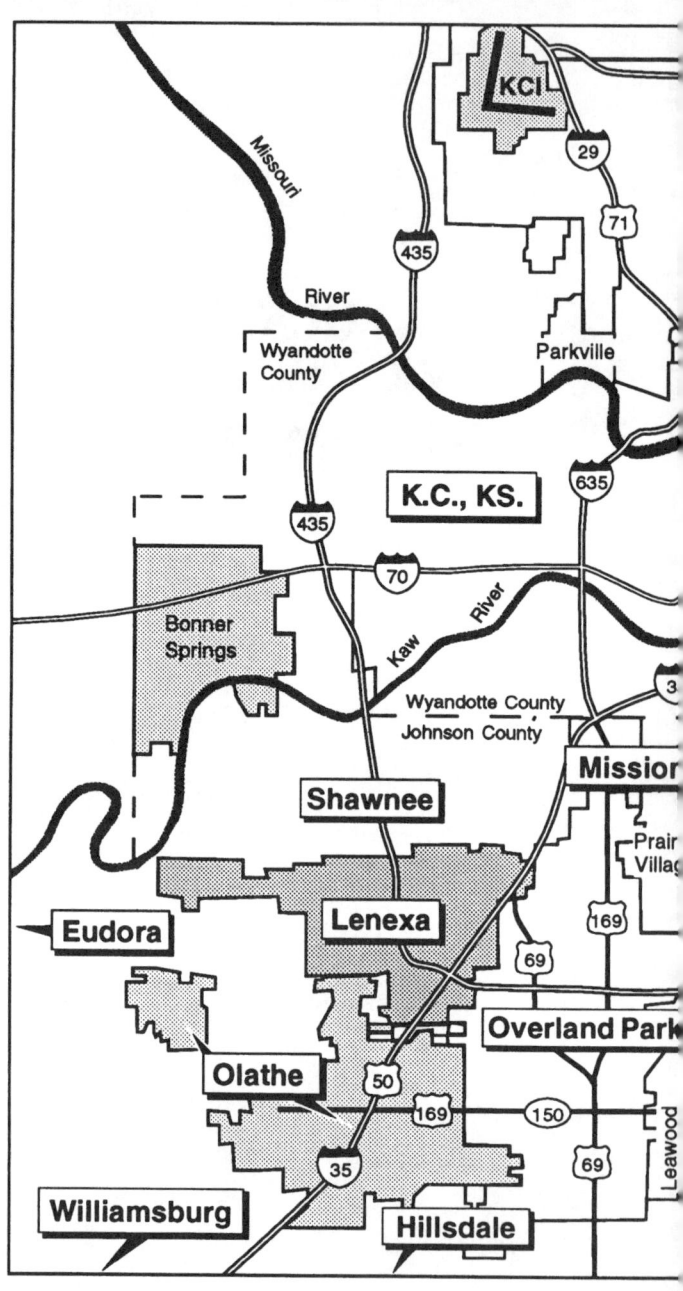

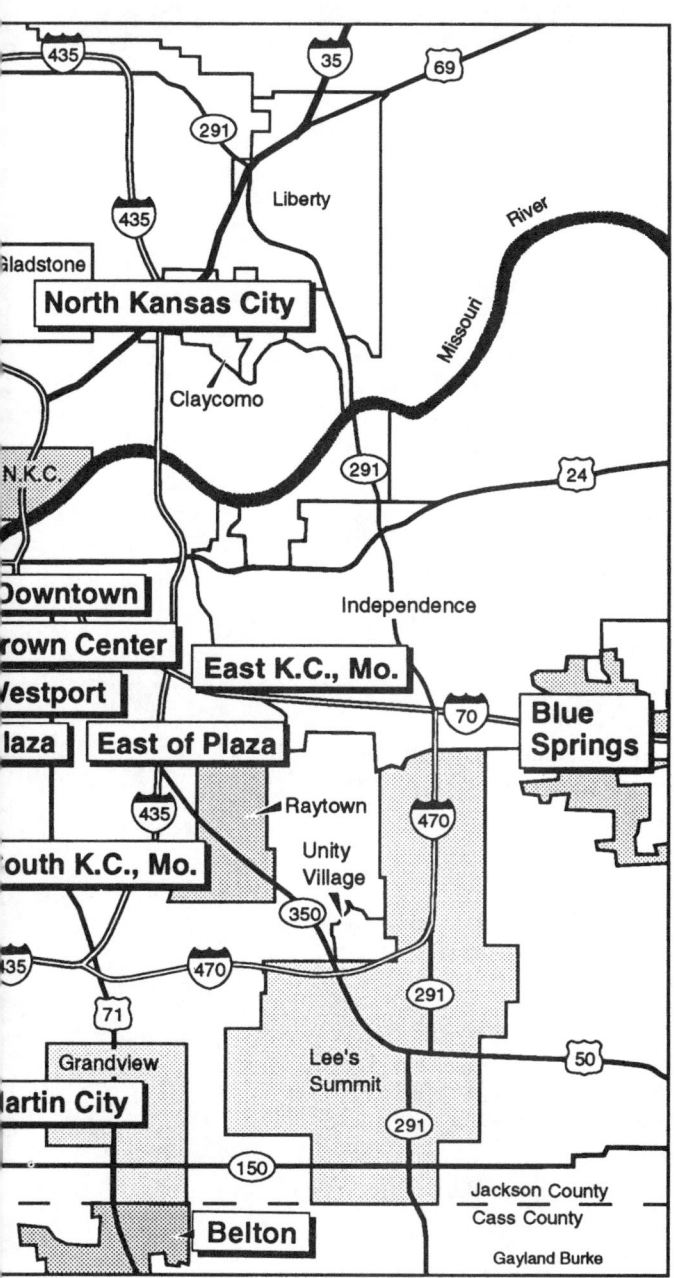

Barbecue Locator 21

KANSAS BARBECUE LOCATOR

Eudora
   CJ's Bar-B-Que 36
Hillsdale
   Hillsdale Bank Bar-B-Q 51
Kansas City
   The Big Q Barbecue 28
   Gates & Sons Bar-B-Q 42
   Porky's Pit Bar-B-Q 71
   Earl Quick's Bar-B-Q 72
   Ricky's Pit Bar-B-Que 76
   Rosedale Barbeque 77
   7th Street Bar-B-Q 83
   Wyandot Bar-B-Q 94
Lenexa
   Longbranch Saloon 64
   Original Smoke Bar-B-Que 68
   Zarda Bar-B-Q 95
Mission
   Coyote Grill 38
   Johnny's Hickory House Bar-B-Q 56
   Werner's Specialty Foods 89
Olathe
   Allen's Bar-B-Que 25
   Gates & Sons Bar-B-Q 42
   Santa Fe Trail Bar-B-Q 81
   Smokin' Joe's BBQ 86
Overland Park
   Boardroom Bar-B-Q 29
   Bodee's Bar-B-Que 31
   Gates & Sons Bar-B-Q 42
   Hayward's Pit Bar-B-Que 47
   Houston's 53
   K.C. Masterpiece Barbecue & Grill 58
   Longbranch Saloon 64
   Wyandot Bar-B-Q 94
Shawnee
   Mark & Jerry's Bar-B-Que Buffet 65
   Rouse's Bar-B-Que 78
Williamsburg
   Guy & Mae's Tavern 46

MISSOURI BARBECUE LOCATOR

Belton
   Snead's Corner Bar-B-Q 88
Blue Springs
   Zarda Bar-B-Q 95
Crown Center Area
   Farmer's B-B-Q 41
   Heartland Bar-B-Que 49
Downtown Kansas City
   Arthur Bryant's Barbecue 35
   Gates & Sons Bar-B-Q 42
   Lil' Jake's Eat It & Beat It 63
   Winslow's City Market Smokehouse 93
East Kansas City
   Gates & Sons Bar-B-Q 42
   Knight's Barbecue 61
   Rustler's Hickory Pit Bar-B-Q 80
East of the Plaza
   Boyd 'n Son Bar-B-Q 33
   Gates & Sons Bar-B-Q 42
Martin City
   Keegan's Bar-B-Q 60
   Smoke Stack Bar-B-Que of Martin City 84
North Kansas City
   Marty's Bar-B-Q 66
Plaza
   Jake Edwards Bar-B-Que 39
   Houston's 53
   K.C. Masterpiece Barbecue and Grill 58
   Longbranch Saloon 64
South Kansas City
   B.B.'s Lawn Side Bar-B-Q 27
   Bodee's Bar-B-Que 31
   O'Toole and Sons Ribs 70
   Ribs 'n Stuff 74
Westport
   Grand Emporium Saloon 44
   Jimmy's Jigger 55
   Westport Bar-B-Que 91

KANSAS CITY 'QUE FROM ALLEN'S TO ZARDA

Allen's Bar-B-Que
1404 E. Santa Fe
Olathe, KS 66061
(913) 780-5400

Cash. Order/pick-up. Sauce bottled for sale.

James Allen learned barbecue from the ground up. Literally. Years ago, Mr. Allen—"a natural-born cook"— taught himself how to barbecue with fence wire and a hand-dug hole in the ground.

Although very young when his father died, Mr. Allen credits him for the inspiration to pursue a career at the pit. Mr. Allen's father had a barbecue counter in his grocery store, where he sold barbecued whole hog to throngs of hungry customers.

From the hole in the ground, James Allen fine-tuned his pitmaster skills in a series of cookers: a galvanized steel washtub, a 55-gallon industrial drum, and a homemade backyard pit with a roof. Today he cooks in a large custom-built steel pit on wheels for catering and in his specially built brick pit at the restaurant.

Regardless of what James Allen cooks in, the result is uniformly delicious. Now, after years of doing barbecue for Kansas City's rich and famous, Mr. Allen's barbecue is available to the general public.

"Our beef," says James Allen, "is tender as mother's love." The same has been said of the ribs at Allen's Bar-B-Que. Staffer Preach Haynes says, "Our ribs are second to none. They're so tender that if you don't have teeth, no problem."

Allen's Bar-B-Que is easy to find. From Kansas City take I-35 south to the first Olathe exit. Go right (west), and Allen's will be on your right, near the Capitol Federal Savings and Loan on the corner. The bright red "Allen's Bar-B-Que" sign is mounted on wooden shingles.

Once inside the limestone brick building, you'll be welcomed with friendly service, a congenial mix of brown padded vinyl booths, Formica-topped tables, photos of notable Allen-catered events, and a portrait of the founder/head pitmaster, James Allen.

The best place to begin at Allen's is the Mix Plate. Get ribs, chicken, and beef with beans and coleslaw. If you've brought a huge appetite, though, start with a Hot Chicken Wing 4-Pack appetizer.

Mr. Allen's Kansas City–style sauce maintains a favorable balance between sweet and tangy. He offers mild, medium, hot, and extra hot. Mr. Allen says his sauce has "a lingering flavor you can't resist." You'll agree. One loyal customer swears that Allen's sauce cured him from an illness. When you take a bottle home, however, keep it in the kitchen instead of the medicine cabinet, to use as a replacement for catsup in meatloaf, on fries, on chips, and even on tacos.

Although new as a restaurant, Allen's Bar-B-Que proudly proclaims itself to be "Kansas City's Best!!!" James Allen, his lovely wife Elsie, Preach Haynes, business manager Donald Franklin, and the entire Allen's Bar-B-Que team is off to an impressive start in that direction.

B.B.'s Lawn Side Bar-B-Q
1205 E. 85th St.
Kansas City, MO 64131
(816) 822-7427

Cash. Table service.

When you make some of the most flavorful pit beans known to humankind and your batter-dipped, spicy, fresh-cut Idaho potato strips are the closest thing to Dixie anywhere north of Mississippi, you're onto something. Add to that some 100% hickory-smoked ribs and rib tips cooked to perfection Kansas City–style and slathered in a sauce that could be called "Rosedale: The Next Generation" (because it has a Rosedale flavor, with more substance and complexity). Add to that a roomy, high-ceilinged, friendly atmosphere for singing or listening to the blues while eating barbecue, and you've found Blues Heaven on Planet Earth. You've also found B.B.'s Lawn Side Bar-B-Q.

Owner Lindsay Shannon has been known for years as a local authority on blues and barbecue. He and his wife Jo have put their pit talents, knowledge, tastes, and management skills together in the creation of this "roadhouse juke joint," as Lindsay calls it.

Along with your ribs and fries at B.B.'s, be sure to get some pit beans. B.B.'s beans are so guaranteed flavorful and excellent that they are worth driving across town just for a bite. They are second to none anywhere on the planet.

The only blues you'll feel like singing at B.B.'s Lawn Side Bar-B-Q are the "I've eaten my ribs and am too full to hold more, but I want more" lament. At B.B.'s the 'Que is true, the blues are blue, and it's all for you.

The Big Q Barbecue
2117 S. 34th St.
Kansas City, KS 66106
(913) 362-6980

Cash. Order/pick-up and table service. Sauce bottled for sale.

The road to The Big Q will take you past houses, rolling hills, and a cemetery reminiscent of a Bonnie and Clyde movie. The resemblance stops when you reach The Big Q, though. Suddenly the setting is modern.

The Big Q's free-standing building could be mistaken for a hamburger emporium at first glance, mostly because of the glassed-in sun room (a rarity among greasehouses). Fortunately, when co-owners/co-pitmasters Rusty Quick and Gary Wright designed The Big Q, they put the pit back far enough that the smoke doesn't smudge the sun room glass.

Customers at The Big Q are loyal and legion. They like the 100% real hickory pit meat that Rusty and Gary excel at cooking. They like the quantity they get for the price. They like the spicy red sauce. They like the friendly service. And they like the opportunity to get to know their local pitmasters.

I judge a barbecue place primarily by how they do with ribs and brisket, and The Big Q gets top honors for both. Throw in some beans, fries, coleslaw and their popular onion rings with oriental flavorings, and you're ready for a barbecue feast that would have made honest citizens of Bonnie and Clyde. When you need some honest barbecue, you won't go wrong with The Big Q.

Boardroom Bar-B-Q
9600 Antioch Rd.
Overland Park, KS 66212
(913) 642-6273

Cash. Table service.

Corporate boardrooms are where executives make big decisions and trivial ones. Here reputations are built, and careers go into orbit or oblivion. Sometimes people take themselves too seriously in there. Sometimes it's important to wake up and smell the bull—get out of the intensity and appreciate some of the finer things of life, such as barbecue.

Boardroom Bar-B-Q is the answer. It will change your thinking about boardrooms and raise your standards for excellence in barbecue. And it will introduce you to new sauces.

Power suits, ties, and briefcases are allowed inside Boardroom—especially at lunchtime on weekdays—but when you're on your own time, arrive in something comfortable. Rib therapy for recovering obsessive executives works better in casual clothing.

Boardroom is easy to find among a cluster of retail stores on the southwest corner of West 95th Street and Antioch. It sports a bright white lighted awning with the restaurant name in green.

Boardroom's location is in its third incarnation as an outstanding barbecue restaurant. First, Hayward Spears started here, followed by former pro basketball player and pro pitmaster, Les Hunter.

Boardroom's interior is designed for an easy flow of customer and staffer traffic. The wall decor, featuring shelves of sauces from all over the world, photos of barbecue events and personalities, a classic color print ("Night of the Living Barbecue," by Kansas City's beloved Cowtown cartoonist, Charlie Podrebarac), and other memorabilia, changes daily as new items appear. What's constant about Boardroom is quality barbecue.

The best way to assert yourself in the pecking order at Boardroom is with a plate of Nuclear Chicken Wings. The very act of ordering them shows that you're not intimidated by power. When you eat them you'll feel empowered—they're hot, but you can handle it.

After the chicken wings, if you're still power-conscious, go for the Chairman of the Board or Chief Executive Officer, with your choice of three or two sliced meats, respectively. At lunchtime you can pick the Power Lunch—half a sandwich with sliced meat of your choice, plus a sampling of Nuclear Chicken Wings or ribs, with bread, fries, and pickles.

If you really want to make a statement about your comfort level with Boardroom Power, get the marinated grilled chicken breast sandwich served with Kansas City's famous Flower of the Flames Raspberry Bar-B-Q Sauce. Eating it doesn't mean you're a wimp. It means you're so comfortable with power that you don't need to be seen in a macho posture with a rib in your mouth and sauce running down your cheeks and forearm. Chicken is as much a state of mind as it is a power metaphor. Chicken is reaching a state of perfection at Boardroom.

And talk about people who are comfortable with power. Boardroom is one of the few places in town with guts enough to showcase other people's sauces. The House Swine—prepared by award-winning pitmasters—is served with your choice of the house sauce or the sauce of the month or both. Plus, with this growing sauce collection, Boardroom is becoming one of the best places in town to get a hint at just how many different barbecue sauces are produced on the planet. If you donate an unopened bottle of sauce that isn't in the Boardroom collection, your Nuclear Chicken Wings are free.

Chief Executive Pitmasters Scott O'Meara, Doug Kellerman, and Mike Godowns invite your investment in a stock market that's easy on your pocketbook and pays high dividends in taste and stress reduction. There's no better place in town to "Escape from the Corporate Bull."

Bodee's Bar-B-Que
Bannister Mall
5620 E. Bannister Rd.
Kansas City, MO 64137
(816) 966-0503

Oak Park Mall
9501 Quivira Rd.
Overland Park, KS 66215
(913) 492-0503

Cash/credit cards. Order/pick-up. Sauce bottled for sale.

Luther Bodee sums up his secret for bodacious barbecue with just two words: slow smokin'. "Slow smokin'," says Bodee, "makes it so good!" He is so right.

Legend has it that young Luther Bodee arrived in Kansas City several years ago with his Texas saddlebags full of secret spices and old family recipes. He had a mind, in a typically Texan manner of humility, to teach Kansas Citians a thing or two about the barbecue method of cooking. Bodee made two concessions to Kansas City tastes. He smokes with hickory instead of mesquite, and he makes his tomato-based Texas sauce sweeter than most Texans prefer it.

It worked. In a matter of a few short years, Luther Bodee has become so successful at pleasing picky Kansas City barbecue palates that his name is synonymous with barbecue in this town. When you say "Bodee," Kansas Citians think "bar-b-que."

Bodee's two free-standing restaurants are designed for efficiency, comfort, and Texas-style conviviality. This isn't a place where you can get your ribs and hide at a dark corner table in rib solitude. Instead, after you've ordered at the counter, paid for it, and found a table or booth while waiting to hear your name called, you'll feel a part of the scene as you sit in the large common dining area. You'll have your own table or booth, and you'll have an acceptable level of privacy, but you'll also feel that sense of community that often happens in the best greasehouses.

Bodee's interior is a Texas swing symphony of real

wood, bricks, red-and-white checkered curtains and tablecloths, and old-fashioned ceiling-fan-globe-lights, punctuated with neon beer and bar-b-que signs. You can read the menu on the wall at the order counter or pick up a printed menu at the entrance to the order line.

The best introduction to Bodee's slow-smokin' pit magic is the special combination plate of beef brisket, pork ribs, link sausage, and your choice of two side orders. By all means get the beans as one of your side orders, and whatever you choose as the other—potato salad, coleslaw, or fries—will not be a disappointment. The disappointment is doing without two of them, so don't disappoint yourself. Order the other two side dishes extra, plus a loaf or half loaf of Bodee's famous Onion Ring Loaf.

Bodee's ribs are so tender and flavorful that they may distract you from trying the other foods on the menu. You'll see the red smoke ring and you'll taste the smoke. Same goes for the beef brisket. These are my two Bodee's favorites. On those rare occasions when I'm in a mood for barbecue chicken, Bodee's never lets me down. The chicken is moist, smoky, and flavorful.

Luther Bodee has an attitude about barbecue sauce: He believes it should be served hot. That's why you won't find bottles of sauce on the tables. You can get all you want, however, by going to the self-service condiment and vittles island in the middle of the dining area, where the sauce is kept hot for customer ladling into serving bowls. Bread, pickles, jalapeño peppers, onion slices, and pico de gallo are also available at the island. Treat yourself to all of it—especially the fresh, delicious pico de gallo. It's there as a fajita garnish, but it's good by itself and on any of the barbecue meats.

Another thing I like about Bodee's is the friendly attitude of the staff. They are there to serve you, and they care about the quality of your dining experience at Bodee's. If you're concerned about getting messy with sauce as you get your hands on Bodee's ribs, they'll provide you with a free "rib bib." And you get free lemon-scented wet-naps without even asking.

After your first visit to Bodee's Bar-B-Que, you'll have an attitude, too. An attitude that barbecue just doesn't get better than Bodee's.

Boyd 'n Son Bar-B-Q
5510 Prospect Ave.
Kansas City, MO 64130
(816) 523-0436

Cash. Order/pick-up. Sauce bottled for sale.

"The people raised so much hell, I *had* to open. They just, everybody called the house and worry you all the time, and said, 'You've *got* to open the place, 'cause we ain't got no place to go.'"

Thankfully, Mr. Otis Boyd, master chef and renowned pitmaster, listened to the neighborhood. A survivor of at least two fires, the simulated brick building with bright cherry-red steel pit doors is back in business.

Mr. Boyd built his own pit. "The pit is what does the job. How that pit performs is what makes your barbecue. My slabs of ribs, they're maroon all the way through, just like ham." The same is true of the lamb breast and lamb shank at Boyd's: It's red to the bone from smoke, without a hint of bitterness. Mr. Boyd is matter-of-fact about the secret to his smoke. "I use anything. Hickory. Oak. Whatever. If you cook with hickory continuously you have to use oak to sweeten it. Hickory gets rough on you."

The Boyd's dining room is clean and functional with no glitz. Textured walls painted light magenta meet simulated wood paneling halfway down from the ceiling. Rows of yellow Formica-topped tables with brown curved wooden booth seats and an Art Deco jukebox occupy the vinyl tile floor.

A certificate from Greg Johnson and Vince Staten, the *Real Barbecue* authors, hangs above the cash register. Boyd's earned their highest honor, "As Good As We've Ever Had." A framed montage of events in the life of the late Dr. Martin Luther King, Jr., also hangs on the wall behind the counter.

Beginners at Boyd's should start with beef brisket, ribs, and sausage. All of the side dishes—potato salad, macaroni salad, baked beans, coleslaw, fries, onion rings, okra, mushrooms, and cauliflower—are made on the premises. "The only thing we've got here that I don't make is catsup and mustard," says Mr. Boyd. The touch of a master chef is evident in each bite.

Boyd's sauce is served liberally with each order, plus a squeeze bottle of warm sauce is offered on the side. It's delicious—not too sweet and not too tangy, with a blend of allspice, nutmeg, cayenne pepper, and other secret spices that form Boyd's unique signature. "Your sauce is 90% of your business. Anybody can cook meat, smoke it and cook it done and make it taste good. It's the sauce that's 90%." Boyd's sauce is available in five varieties: Old Original, Hot, Smoky, Onion, and Horseradish. Old Original, slathered on hot, red-to-the-bone lamb breast, is one of my all-time favorites.

At Boyd's you'll get a taste of the barbecue that helped make Kansas City famous. "As far as real barbecue: This is as real as you're ever gonna' get in your life."

Arthur Bryant's Barbecue
1727 Brooklyn Ave.
Kansas City, MO 64127
(816) 231-1123

Cash. Cafeteria-style order/pick-up. Sauce bottled for sale.

Arthur Bryant's is steeped in myth, legend, and hype, and has been called "world class," "the choice of presidents," and "mecca" by thousands of barbecue aficionados. So when first-timers open the aluminum-framed glass door and step inside, walk on linoleum past plain Formica-topped tables and white textured walls adorned with magazine and news reviews, cartoons, photos, and a portrait of Mr. Bryant himself, they often remark, "This is it?!"

You'll be struck by how unpretentious the place is. Mr. Bryant called it a "greasehouse." Nothing more. Nothing less.

As you proceed to the cafeteria line at the back and read the menu on the wall, you'll reach the black ornamental iron porch railing in front of the order window and a friendly pitmaster will ask, "What'll you have?" Most people reply, "Beef and fries." You can't go wrong with that. True to his Texas upbringing, Arthur Bryant excelled in cooking beef brisket. He also turned out some very respectable barbecue pork spareribs.

Today at Arthur Bryant's you'll get delicious barbecue much the same as the founder prepared it. And the freshly cut potatoes, deep-fried in 400 degrees of pure lard, are unequaled anywhere.

The grainy, paprika-laden, tomato-vinegar-based sauce, accented with curry seasonings and cayenne pepper, is an instant hit with some, an acquired taste for most.

Note the big bottles of sauce aging in the window sills. Be sure to buy a smaller sized bottle to take home. You may wake up late at night craving a taste of it. It's reasonably priced and wrapped in butcher paper just the way Mr. Bryant sold it.

You'll leave Arthur Bryant's with a new respect for grease.

CJ's Bar-B-Que
726 Main St.
Eudora, KS 66025
(913) 542-3182

Cash. Order/pick-up. Sauce available for sale.

Find a town where barbecue is sold from prime retail space on Main Street, and you've found a town with its priorities in the right order. Eudora, Kansas, is such a place. Find a man who can watch his job and career literally go up in smoke, and then make a new career out of smoke, and you've found a true American entrepreneur. Chris "CJ" Deay is such a man.

By name, CJ's Bar-B-Que is a newcomer to Eudora, but as a continuation of the former Bichelmeyer's Bar-B-Que, 726 Main has been a popular barbecue pit stop in the surrounding area since 1985. The two-story red brick building that houses CJ's was originally a saddle shop. Since the turn of the century the building has been home to numerous restaurants, but it met its destiny as a barbecue restaurant when Ray and Sandy Bichelmeyer set up shop. Chris Deay, owner and head pitmaster of CJ's Bar-B-Que, formerly was a part-time employee of Bichelmeyer's, back when he was assistant manager at the lumberyard that went up in smoke. The Bichelmeyers happened to be ready to sell when Chris was ready to buy. Ray Bichelmeyer trained Chris in the art of pit smoking and sauce making and in restaurant management. Ray is a good teacher and Chris is a good learner, and the barbecue-consuming public is the happy beneficiary of all that education.

Several roads lead to Eudora. The main route is from the Highway 10 Jayhawk Freeway toward Lawrence to the Eudora exit. A more scenic route takes you along two-lane roads through DeSoto and past Linwood to the county road known unofficially as Eudora Road. Get a map and call CJ's for the best directions from your location. When you reach Main Street Eudora, you'll find CJ's Bar-B-Que on the east side of the street toward the north end of Main. The white and green logo painted on the storefront window proudly proclaims, "CJ's Bar-B-Que."

The building that houses CJ's on the ground floor and a Masonic meeting room on the top could have served well in an Edward Hopper painting, had Mr. Hopper ever visited Eudora. The resemblance to Hopper's paintings ends, though, when you step inside CJ's. No "Night Hawks" setting here, and no old-fashioned general store or saddle shop decor to echo the building's past. Just plain, peach-colored sheetrock walls, gray linoleum tile floor, a set of green padded booths along the north wall, a row of four-seater tables down the middle, and a row of long tables jutting out from the south wall. New fluorescent-lighted acoustical tile hides the original 15-foot ceiling.

CJ's burnt ends and the beef brisket is some of the best I've ever tasted. It meets the no sauce test, as it can easily stand alone without seasoning of any kind. The sauce is thick, sweet, lightly flavored with herbs and spices, and bright red. It's really not necessary with meat this good. Use it with your curly fries.

The ribs, too, can stand alone. They are smoked to the bone, tender and flavorful. No rub applied; no rub needed. And how about the turkey breast? Real "muscle meat," as Chris says. And you'll say it's real good. Same goes for the pork and the chicken. I didn't try the ham.

Besides curly fries, Chris also offers home-style beans flavored with hot CJ's barbecue sauce (it's on the mild end of the hot scale), potato salad, and pickles.

CJ's barbecue is about as close to primal as you can get: smoke, fire, and meat. You owe it to yourself to give it a try. The great barbecue, the small-town atmosphere, and the friendly service will make you glad you journeyed to this town with its priorities in the right order and this pitmaster-entrepreneur whose career is in smoke.

Coyote Grill
Mission Shopping Center (upper level)
4843 Johnson Dr.
Mission, KS 66205
(913) 362-3333

Cash/credit cards. Table service.

Coyote doesn't represent itself as a barbecue restaurant, but their barbecue ribs are worth your attention. Marinated, smoked in an electric smoker, flash-grilled, and sauced with the refreshingly distinctive Coyote house barbecue sauce, these ribs could bring home some prizes. On the menu they are called "Oh, Baby, KC Ribs," but each time I've eaten there the ribs are spareribs instead of baby backs. No problem. The taste is excellent.

Most of Coyote's cuisine, as the name implies, is Southwestern. Grilled chicken breast is featured in a variety of dishes. The salads and soups are fantastic and the desserts are loaded with richness and flavor.

Coyote's presentation, architecturally and on the plates, rivals places in New York, Dallas, and L.A., where your tip total could exceed the cost of the entire Coyote experience.

Jake Edwards Bar-B-Que
5107 Main St.
Kansas City, MO 64112
(816) 531-8878

Cash. Table service.

Jake Edwards was an almost larger-than-life legend in Kansas City barbecue, and thousands mourned his passing. With a legacy like that, it takes courage to run a barbecue restaurant with the name Jake Edwards on it. Mike Daniels has the courage. Self-taught, with a hint or two from Jake when he bought the place, Mike has continued a Kansas City barbecue tradition on Main Street that does tribute and justice to the Jake Edwards legacy.

Jake Edwards is easy to find from the Country Club Plaza. Just go south on Main, up the hill, and follow your nose when the hickory smoke hits it. It's an easy walk or a short drive. There's free parking at the curb and in the back.

Jake Edwards Bar-B-Que isn't large. The booths along the north and south walls and the rows of tables in the middle are filled with devout barbecue aficionados at lunchtime and dinnertime. To be among them, plan to arrive before or after the rush, or be prepared to wait awhile for seating. Worth the wait, it's no exaggeration to say that Jake Edwards Bar-B-Que is truly one of Kansas City's best. On the basis of the quality of the barbecue—especially the ribs, beef, and turkey breast—the quantity of the servings, the prices, the comfortable and congenial atmosphere, and the friendly service, I rate Jake Edwards Bar-B-Que as one of my top favorites. And that's without even mentioning the fries. I always get an order of regular fries and an order of sweet potato fries to eat with the Jake Edwards 'Que. You don't need catsup, as the Jake Edwards sauce is good enough to put on anything, especially the meat and the fries. It's brown, tangy-sweet, spicy with powdered cumin and other flavors, and complicated enough to stand out on its own among the many local sauces. Unfortunately, though, Mike doesn't bottle it for sale.

Another thing I take pleasure in at Jake Edwards is

the presentation of the food, which arrives in individual round metal serving trays, on white waxed paper. The fries come in diner-style plastic oval baskets lined with the same paper. A cold brew, iced tea, or a soda rounds out your order.

Save room, though, for one more item: a Jake Edwards brownie. They're at the counter in the back, and few customers, when paying their bill, can resist buying one.

Mike Daniels may not be as well known as Jack Daniel, but his commitment to excellence emulates him.

Farmer's B-B-Q
315 W. Pershing Rd.
(Main Post Office)
Kansas City, MO 64108

Cash. Sauce bottled for sale.

Farmer's B-B-Q brings the down-on-the-farm tastes of 100% hickory-smoked barbecue to Kansas City's main post office every weekday. "Curbside 'Que" best depicts this movable barbecue feast. Owner/pitmasters Daniel and Sue Gardner—a good name for proprietors of a place called Farmer's—serve generous portions of ribs, beef, ham, real turkey breast, and Polish sausage at unbelievably generous prices.

The popular "Farmer's Jumbo" sandwich is your choice of over one pound of meats and sells for only $5.00. A regular Farmer's customer feeds herself and her three children with a Jumbo Combo once a week. Homemade coleslaw, potato salad, or macaroni salad are good on the side. The slightly tangy, tomato-based sauce comes from a secret family recipe handed down from Sue's grandmother. It adds just the right complement to the 'Que.

When you're on the move or if you work in the area, be sure to catch Farmer's. Don or Sue will talk catering with you at (816) 461-8934 after 8:00 p.m.

Gates & Sons Bar-B-Q Headquarters
4707 The Paseo
Kansas City, MO 64110
(816) 923-0900

2001 W. 103rd Terr.
Overland Park, KS 66206
(913) 383-1752

1026 State Ave.
Kansas City, KS 66102
(913) 621-1134

1221 Brooklyn Ave.
Kansas City, MO 64127
(816) 483-3880

10440 E. 40 Hwy.
Kansas City, MO 64055
(816) 353-5880

215 N. Rawhide Dr.
Olathe, KS 66062
(913) 764-6210

Cash. Order/pick-up. Sauce bottled for sale throughout the metropolitan area.

You can't say "Kansas City barbecue" without saying "Gates." The Gates presence, historically and in today's competitive market, is big, powerful, and here to stay. Hundreds, possibly thousands, of Kansas Citians can't go for a full week without a taste of Gates barbecue to sustain them. Former Kansas Citians and others who have visited K.C. and been hooked by the Gates taste and mystique have ribs and beef and sauce flown to their homes and offices on a regular basis. It scares me to think what would happen to the mental health of a substantial portion of our citizenry if there were no more Gates & Sons

Bar-B-Q. Happily, we needn't waste emotional energy with such worries.

Gates & Sons Bar-B-Q will imprint a visual memory of a man in full tuxedo in your mind, and an auditory memory of the phrase, "Hi, may I help you?" You get the visuals and the question the moment you step inside, often before you've found and glanced at the menu. If you pride yourself on instant response, practice saying, "Yes. Beef and fries, please." Or, "Yes. Short end, beans, and fries, please." It's best, though, to take as much time as you wish to study the menu on the wall behind the order counter, and get what sounds good to you.

To my taste, barbecue doesn't get any better than a Gates beef sandwich with freshly cut fries. You'll find other Gates regulars who swear by the ribs. Try both and make your own decision. Eat your way through the rest of Gates menu, trying something new on each visit. This is one of the very few places in town offering barbecue mutton, for example.

Gates barbecue sauce tastes like a blend of tomato sauce, ketchup, powdered cumin seeds, celery salt, cayenne pepper, and some other secret ingredients. Available mild, hot, and extra hot, it makes a savory, uncomplicated statement to your palate. The extra hot holds title to "Best Barbecue Sauce on the Planet, 1991" from the American Royal International Barbecue Sauce Contest. It complements Gates meats and enjoys a very loyal nationwide following. For a different twist on the Gates signature taste, try the Polynesian-style sauce.

As you've noted by the list of addresses above, Gates & Sons Bar-B-Q is all over town. You won't be believed if you live here and haven't tried it, or if you visit here and haven't tried it. Everyone has an opinion about Gates & Sons Bar-B-Q, so you'd best be "Struttin' with Gates."

Grand Emporium Saloon
3832 Main St.
Kansas City, MO 64111
(816) 531-1504

Cash. Order/pick-up. Sauce bottled for sale.

From the outside, the Grand Emporium could easily pass as a few feet of concrete jungle in New York's Upper West Side. The brick buildings, storefronts, urban sidewalk, pedestrian and vehicular traffic, and neon signs will feel familiar to hikers who have walked Broadway from Zabar's to Columbia University. If you take time to look at the fliers and posters advertising upcoming and past events at the Grand Emporium, you'll know that here, in this little slice of Kansas City, the richness of cultural diversity is alive and well.

At the Grand Emporium the music is fabulously eclectic, and the ribs and red and white create a Cajun symphony of flavors that go beyond good to simply amazing.

The semidarkness inside the Grand Emporium sets a mood of anticipation and makes the size of this music-barbecue-booze palace feel small and friendly. To your left is the bar. Food and drink counters for standing patrons line the walls beyond the bar. Neon lights, music posters, and other memorabilia cover the walls. A few rows of folding chairs face the small stage around the corner to your right. Before you get to the stage, if you're at the Grand Emporium to try the barbecue, you'll put your order in at the counter near the bar.

Most nights at Grand Emporium's food counter you'll be greeted by "Amazing Grace" herself, head pitmaster Grace Harris. The popularity of Grace's barbecue and her amazing sauces and seasonings has elevated her to living legend status in Kansas City. It hasn't gone to her head, though, because she's still absorbed in reaching even greater heights. Her sauce has won "Best in the U.S.A." at the American Royal International Barbecue Sauce Contest, and her baste has won "Best on the Planet." Grace says she can do even better than that, and you can bet she's going to prove it.

You won't likely have time to visit with Grace. The Grand Emporium food counter is understandably busy, so when it's your turn you'll have time to order, pay, get your food, and make room for the next customer behind you. Get ribs with a side of red and white. If you're with a companion, share the order of ribs—you'll get two each—and get your own individual serving of Cajun-style red beans and rice. The ribs are pricey, but you'll feel O.K. about it when you take the first bite. Grace seasons and smokes her ribs to perfection. The meat won't fall off the bone, but it's tender enough to reach 8 on a scale of 1 to 10.

It's a challenge to find a place to enjoy your food at the Grand Emporium. The dining mode is mostly lap-top or stand-up, so if you're there for the food only, it's best to get carryout and dine in the comfort of your car, hotel room, or home.

If you like music and barbecue, plan to buy a ticket for the featured musical entertainment, eat ribs, and enjoy yourself. On any given evening at the Grand Emporium the featured musicians may do zydeco, rock, blues, reggae, country-western, or avant garde sounds. Continuity is maintained by the regular house band, "Little Hatch and the House Rockers."

Since the Grand Emporium, thanks to owners George Meyers and Roger Naber, features an unbelievable array of the world's best musical talent, you stand a good chance of counting your evening there as one of those unforgettably pleasant memories to call upon when the blues knock at your door. One of my most memorable Grand Emporium evenings featured Chicago blues legend Buddy Guy. Another was spent with singer-songwriters Townes Van Zandt and Robert Earl Keen, Jr.

Take your feet to 3832 Main Street for some of the best rib and music therapy in town.

Guy & Mae's Tavern
119 W. Williams St.
(next to fire station)
Williamsburg, KS 66095
(913) 746-8830

Cash. Order/pick-up. Sauce bottled for sale.

The late Guy Kesner was publicly recognized as the brew and rib king of Kansas in 1985, when Dave Kratzer, editor of *KS. Magazine,* proclaimed Guy & Mae's Tavern to be "The Best BarBieCue Joint in Kansas."

Williamsburg is not in metropolitan Kansas City. It's not even in the suburban outer limits of Kansas City. So why is a place featuring a sauce as sweet as spaghetti sauce, and so far away from Kansas City that it takes at least an hour to get there, in a book about Kansas City barbecue? Because the G & M tradition of tender rib slabs and sweet sauce has attracted thousands of Kansas Citians over recent years. Guy and Mae's is also a favorite, must-eat-there destination of thousands of Topekans, Jayhawkers from Lawrence, and Wildcats from Manhattan.

Guy and Mae's children and their spouses, with technical assistance from Mae, continue to make sauce and smoke ribs exactly as Guy did it. Guy's secret sauce is, to my taste buds, a close accidental blended cousin to Paul Newman's Spaghetti Sauce and Rudolph's Bar-B-Que Sauce of St. Paul, Minnesota. Its sweetness, laced with Guy's secret "hookey poo" blend of herbs and spices, is the right complement to G & M's fall off-the-bones smoked ribs.

Order one slab of ribs per couple, with beans, coleslaw, and super-cold brew or soda on the side. The ribs are served on aluminum foil and newspapers in true greasehouse style.

There's a long bar with stools and a row of booths along the wall in this unpretentious tavern on the Kansas prairie. Music is by way of jukebox country-western songs. The food is so good at Guy and Mae's that you'll be singing "I don't wanna go home" when it's time to leave. Get a slab to go. You'll thank yourself tomorrow.

Hayward's Pit Bar-B-Que
11051 Antioch Rd.
Overland Park, KS 66210
(913) 451-8080

Cash/credit cards. Table service. Carryout order counter. Sauce bottled for sale.

There's only one Hayward's Pit Bar-B-Que, and that's how it's likely to stay. In the tradition of the late Arthur Bryant and many of the other greatest pitmasters on earth, Hayward Spears believes that attending to the daily details of running a quality barbecue restaurant bears a lot of resemblance to marriage. Monogamy is all one man and one woman have time for if it's going to be done right.

Hayward Spears does it right. He knows barbecue. He knows what his customers want, and he knows how to stay the course in maintaining high standards in taste, generous quantities, and reasonable prices.

When Hayward's outgrew its former location at Antioch and 95th Street, Mr. Spears decided to move south to the growth corridor along College Boulevard. The dining capacity at the new location easily quadrupled. You'll see why when you get there.

The first thing you'll notice when you arrive at Hayward's is how busy it is, outside and inside. A good measure of just *how* busy is the customer count, meat tonnage, sauce gallonage, and wood usage in an average year. Hayward's reportedly serves over a half million customers in an average year, selling over 400 tons of meat and over 10,000 gallons of sauce. It takes over 100 cords of hickory to barbecue the meat.

Lesser pitmasters could get lost in the magnitude and myriad details attendant on the success of an operation such as Hayward's Pit Bar-B-Que. Not Hayward Spears. He knows what needs to be done and he knows how to get it done. When your plate of ribs arrives from Hayward's kitchen, it is presented exactly to Mr. Spears's standards. Same goes for everything else on the menu. Attention to detail. Consistency. Quality. This is what you'll see at Hayward's. You'll also see Hayward Spears.

He's active all over the restaurant—greeting customers, expediting orders, bussing tables, attending to details. He knows at least 3,000 of his regular customers by name.

The restaurant itself is designed to fit the neighborhood. The neighborhood is upscale, affluent, corporate. Generic greasehouse architecture and decor wouldn't fit here. Hayward's brick and glass structure and steakhouse decor of wood paneling, carpeting, plants, and comfortable seating does fit here.

For me it's a toss-up at Hayward's as to what's the best food on the menu. I usually choose beef or ribs. The sausage is good, too. All of the meat at Hayward's has the heavenly taste of real pitsmoked barbecue. His sauce brings out the flavor even more, and it doesn't distract you with sweetness. For sweetness, save room for Hayward's sweet potato pie. There's none better in Kansas City.

Hayward's Pit Bar-B-Que is another of the famous Kansas City restaurants to put on your must-try list. If there's a wait when you arrive and your schedule doesn't allow for waiting, go to the carryout room. You'll get fast and friendly service. Accommodating your needs is another detail that doesn't escape Mr. Spears.

Heartland Bar-B-Que
Crown Center Shops (Level 1)
2450 Grand Ave.
Kansas City, MO 64108
(816) 426-1123

Cash/credit cards. Order/pick-up. Sauce bottled for sale.

There are lots of good things to be said for Hallmark's very best gift to Kansas City. But from a swine diner's perspective, the greasehouse gold in the Crown Center complex of retail stores, hotels, restaurants, offices, and entertainment centers is on the ground level of the Crown Center Shops. Here barbecue lovers and sauce collectors will feel like they've found the true heart of the Kansas City called "Cowtown Central" by the *Real Barbecue* authors Vince Staten and Greg Johnson. Although the designation "Heartland" for the marketplace of retail stores and the barbecue restaurant is meant to signify Kansas City's geographic location in the heart of the U.S.A., it is also a place that gladdens the heart of anyone who has a serious love for barbecue.

Guests at the Westin Crown Center Hotel and the Hyatt Regency Crown Center have an easy stroll to Heartland Bar-B-Que. When the weather is good, take the outdoor route. Other times, come through the Westin Crown Center lobby—accessed via the new skywalk from the Hyatt Regency. If you're staying somewhere else, every cab driver in town knows how to reach this famous place. If you're in your own vehicle, enter the Crown Center Garage for three hours of free parking. (Remember to bring your parking ticket for validation at any of the Crown Center shops or restaurants.)

Once inside, when you reach Level 1, look for a pink, neon-lighted, heart-shaped sign. It's mounted on a stucco wall outside the entrance to Heartland Bar-B-Que. The name, too, is in neon lights.

Heartland isn't a fancy place, nor is it glitzy. The floor is standard restaurant kitchen terra-cotta tile. The vinyl tablecloths are patterned with the red-and-white checks familiar to millions of Heartland homemakers.

The wooden chairs hold comfortable, padded vinyl seat cushions. The order counter roof sports wooden slat panels stamped "USDA" in rectangular borders.

My favorites at Heartland are the beef sandwich with fries and coleslaw or the ribs with a side order of beans. The hickory-smoke flavor of the meat is very gentle—the slight kiss of smoke familiar to mid-Southerners. The sauce has just the right balance of sweetness and tanginess, with a peppery accent. The counter help puts exactly the right amount of sauce on the meat, but if you want more of this delicious concoction, it's available on the counter opposite the serving counter. The sauce goes well with the fries, too. If you're dieting, or just not hungry for beef or pork, get the chicken. It's real chicken, like Heartland grandmothers raised on the farm, and it's deliciously flavored with the same gentle kiss of smoke.

After dining at Heartland Bar-B-Que, be sure to buy a bottle of Heartland Bar-B-Que Sauce to take home. Then go to the stores nearby and select some other local and out-of-town varieties. Sauce lovers are thrilled by this place. There is no better souvenir of Kansas City than a bottle of authentic Kansas City barbecue sauce, and there is no better selection in town than the selection at Crown Center. Get some for yourself and for the people on your gift list. If you have to travel light, select your sauces and have them shipped home. And don't make yourself choose from among the local brands—KC Baron of Barbecue, Kansas City Classic, Chef Dan's, Flower of the Flames, Bodee's, and Arthur Bryant's, to name a few. Get them all. Throw in some rib rubs, too—or get sauce, rubs, and a great cookbook in the "Passion Pack."

After all that shopping, reward yourself with another helping of Heartland Bar-B-Que. If you'd rather have dessert, there's lots of that to choose from, too, in several nearby sweet shops.

Heartland Bar-B-Que. Shopping. More barbecue. Dessert. Could anything be more American or more satisfying?

Hillsdale Bank Bar-B-Q
Church & Frisco Sts.
Hillsdale, KS 66036
(913) 783-4333

Open Thurs.–Sun. Cash. Table service. Sauce packaged for sale.

Kansas City visitors who are new to the Midwest and want to get an authentic, nostalgic taste of small-town, rural, Heartland America should put a visit to Hillsdale Bank Bar-B-Q number one on their swine dining itinerary. Same goes for urban prairie dwellers who want a refreshing break from the crunch of skyscrapers and the monotony of suburban sprawl. It's 35 miles from Kansas City, and worth investing in the time and fuel to get there. Call ahead for directions from your location. In general, the route from Kansas City is by way of I-35 south beyond Olathe to 56 Highway, then Highway 169 beyond Spring Hill to the Hillsdale/Wagstaff exit. Go right at the exit; turn left at the sign of the pig before you get to the railroad tracks. You'll see and smell this unpretentious little establishment, which promises all customers, "You can bank on our ribs"—a Fine Swining Licensed Informal Contract (FSLIC) that you can trust.

Architecturally, Hillsdale Bank Bar-B-Q is a simple brick-walled rectangle adjoined by a makeshift wood-framed building to an old railroad car converted into an extra dining area. The connecting building, complete with a working pot-bellied stove, serves as an entrance, reception area, carryout counter, server station, and kitchen. Hillsdale Bank Bar-B-Q only seated 30 when it first opened. Seating capacity has now grown to 100. Greg banks the coals, tends the pit, and manages the kitchen while Donna serves as hostess and expediter in the reception and dining areas.

The mood and attire here are casual. Farmers, ranchers, blue collar workers, and city slickers give a comfortable feel of cultural diversity. The most popular dinner plate is the House Specialty, featuring a reasonably priced plate of two ribs and your choice of two other meats such as beef, pork, ham, turkey, and sausage. I recommend the ribs, beef, and pork with slaw and fries. You can't go wrong with the beans and onion rings either. Order them all!

When your disposable plate, loaded with meat and side dishes, arrives, you'll notice immediately that head pitmaster Greg Beverlin has been around the barbecue pit a few times. These ribs are lean, smoked red to the bone, and so tender they pull easily off the bones. The slightly crispy outside, smoky, not bitter, flavor, and no hint of a rub makes these ribs as close to authentic, true barbecue as can be found anywhere. When you take time off the ribs to try the pork and the beef, you'll not be disappointed. The pork could put a smile on any Memphian and the beef could put a smile on any Texan. All three—ribs, pork, and beef—can stand alone on flavor. They needn't stand alone on flavor at the Bank, however, because the sauce is worthy of the meat and helps it pamper your palate. The Bank sauce is Kansas City sweet, Tennessee tangy, and Texas smoky. It's good enough to take home.

If you're with a group, order from the rest of the menu and share a little of everything. The sausage is a typical Texas hot link, so be prepared for a tingling bite on your lips as an aftertaste. Dieters will love the chicken—moist, smoky, and good for you. The turkey has an ever-so-slight kiss of smoke.

The Hillsdale Bank Bar-B-Q is fun, unpretentious, good eating. Donna Beverlin summed it up best when she said, "It's delicious food, a great country drive, and a nostalgic atmosphere."

Houston's
The Plaza
4640 Wornall Rd.
Kansas City, MO 64112
(816) 561-8542

7111 W. 95th St.
Overland Park, KS 66212
(913) 642-0630

Cash/credit cards. Table service.

So many Kansas Citians have told me of their love for the ribs at Houston's that I just had to find out why. How is it, I asked myself, that a corporate chain headquartered in Atlanta could get even a passing nod from residents of one of the most famous barbecue cities on earth?

When I stepped inside, my suspicions heightened. Especially when I passed a brass sign advising me that proper attire is required. Fortunately for me, the hostess took no offense at my white sweatshirt with "3rd Annual Jack Daniel's World Championship Invitational Barbecue, 1991, Lynchburg, TN" splashed across the chest in red, orange, and black.

I saw businessmen in power suits and people of varying ages in the jeans–casual attire of the '90s. Some of the women looked Fifth Avenue New Yorkish, others like Yalies on spring break. Overalls and gimme caps were conspicuously absent.

I continued to wonder, "Why *these* ribs?" as I waited for my order. Of the side dish choices ranging from fries to creamy coleslaw to skillet beans to couscous, I chose the latter two, mostly because no one else in town serves skillet beans and couscous with their ribs. I was curious.

When my order was up and ready for delivery, my suspense grew so intense that I almost met my friendly server halfway as she walked toward me in her white blouse and black skirt, past bricks and brass, mahogany and glass, burgundy Naugahyde, smoke, and mirrors. With a smile she placed the ribs before me and said, "Enjoy."

Houston's gets an A on rib presentation. The oval white ceramic platter is rib perfect. The ramekin of skillet beans, scoop of couscous, and parsley garnish reflect care and attention to detail. Even more importantly, the ribs emitted a smoky aroma. Before taking the first bite, I looked in vain for smoke rings. I picked up a rib and the meat fell off. That's tender. Then I picked up the meat that fell off the bone and I took a bite. It was tender, flavorful, had the right amount of smokiness, was sauced to complement, and, as my Georgia barbecue buddy Billy "Shug" Powell is prone to say about his own barbecue, made me think "Take me now, Lord, because heaven can't be any better than this!"

Kansas City's praise of Houston's ribs is well deserved. Any cowpoke with a cauldron, a campfire, and a bottle of Cattleman's Barbecue Sauce couldn't do ribs better than Houston's.

Jimmy's Jigger
1823 W. 39th St.
Kansas City, MO 64111
(816) 753-2444

Cash/credit cards. Table service.

Jimmy's Jigger has some of the looks of a sports bar—TVs and so on—but it stakes its identity on blues, booze, and barbecue in a brick and wood multilevel neighborhood bar setting.

Jimmy doesn't hold court here on a daily and nightly basis as he did before he sold the place, but he does make an occasional appearance. For as long as there's a Jimmy's Jigger his presence will be felt here. And not only because of the name and the neon Jimmy silhouette and the poster-sized black-and-whites of Jimmy in amusing postures on the wall. Jimmy lives in the memory and admiration of the many loyal Jigger regulars who keep coming back.

Terry Ray and Lloyd Stark are the new owners of Jimmy's Jigger, and they have continued its BBQ tradition. The hickory/apple smoke taste of the barbecue achieved here is the best. There's no hint of bitterness, as can happen with fruitwood smoke.

Jimmy's tomato-based, sweet, flavorful sauce will stick to your meat and make you cry "I love Kansas City!" whether you're a native urban prairie dweller or a first-time visitor.

The coleslaw at the Jigger is creamy and sweet with a slight pineapple accent. And don't pass up the award-winning pit beans or the homemade potato chips and fries. Kansas City's Boulevard Beer is kept on tap here, along with a good selection of domestic and imported brews, too.

Once you've tried the barbecue and ambience at Jimmy's Jigger, you'll often be back for more.

Johnny's Hickory House Bar-B-Q
5959 Broadmoor Dr.
Mission, KS 66202
(913) 432-0777

Cash/credit cards. Table service. Sauce bottled for sale.

I admit to boldfaced bias when it comes to Johnny's Hickory House Bar-B-Q. Johnny White is my neighborhood pitmaster. I eat a lot of barbecue from Johnny's, and I rate it as some of the best in the world.

Johnny's is easy to find from Johnson Drive. Turn south on Broadmoor, and you'll see the place on the northeast corner. Johnny took over what used to be a pizza parlor several years ago and converted it into a hickory house. With due respect to pizza lovers, the quality of food coming out of that once-a-pizza-parlor building since Johnny moved in is beyond comparison. Johnny's isn't just another barbecue restaurant. It's one of the best. Johnny's pitmaster skills, especially with ribs and beef, is what makes his Hickory House so good.

Inside this red brick greasehouse a Western theme prevails. Prints of cowpokes and Native Americans, bits of cowboy gear, and miscellaneous other items adorn the simulated wood-paneled walls. The order area is tiled, the dining areas are carpeted. Seating provides a comfortable choice among booths and tables. The fireplace gives the main dining room a homey feel.

On the wall to your left as you stand at the order counter Johnny has assembled some trophies, photos, and mementos of the Little League sports teams that the Hickory House has sponsored. This symbol of Johnny's active involvement in the community makes a modest statement compared to the many unsung and little known acts of kindness that he has perpetrated.

Johnny's hickory-smoked barbecue alone is one of the greatest acts of kindness he does for Kansas City seven days a week. The Hickory House ribs melt in your mouth and jolt your taste buds into ecstasy. You'll savor the hickory smoke and you'll appreciate Johnny's bright red sauce; its gentle bite of red pepper and seasonings suggest Rosedale, but bear Johnny's own signature.

The beef sandwich at Johnny's shares the same qualities as the ribs: smoke rings, tenderness, and superb flavor. I seldom order anything other than ribs or beef (or both) at Johnny's because they're some of my very favorites in Kansas City. And with barbecue as good as this, I don't lament Johnny's use of frozen crinkle-cut fries. In fact, I like them. Johnny says all of his other customers do, too.

Support your local pitmaster. And please support mine, too. Give Johnny's a try. He says the Hickory House is the best-kept secret in Johnson County. If so, it's a secret waiting to be whispered all over the planet!

K.C. Masterpiece Barbecue & Grill
10985 Metcalf Ave.
Overland Park, KS 66210
(913) 345-1199

4747 Wyandotte St. (The Plaza)
Kansas City, MO 64112
(816) 531-3332

Cash/credit cards. Table service. Sauce sold in supermarkets nationwide.

The "S" in the name K.C. Masterpiece does double-duty. It makes the word *masterpiece* complete, and it suggests the big "S" word that summarizes a particular corporate history in one word: "Success."

The barbecue sauce that shares the name of this restaurant chain was developed in a suburban Kansas City home kitchen. It became nationally available and internationally famous less than 10 years after its commercial entry into the extremely competitive barbecue sauce marketplace. Now K.C. Masterpiece sauce is owned and marketed by the Kingsford Company with assistance from Dr. Rich Davis, originator of the sauce and founder of the K.C. Masterpiece Barbecue & Grill.

The K.C. Masterpiece Barbecue & Grill restaurants represent Phase II of the Davis family mission to introduce the citizens of Planet Earth to the primal pleasure of eating top-quality slow-smoked barbecue and pecan-grilled meats. The original restaurant on Metcalf in Overland Park, Kansas, is where the initiative began. Its popularity with Kansas Citians, tourists, and visiting executives was immediate when the doors first opened in 1987 and hasn't stopped since. As word has spread about the quality of the food and dining experience at K.C. Masterpiece, literally thousands of swine diners have proclaimed it to be their Number One Favorite Barbecue Restaurant. The same phenomenon has happened in the St. Louis metropolitan area, where K.C. Masterpiece Barbecue & Grill operates two very successful restaurants.

The new K.C. Masterpiece Barbecue & Grill on the Country Club Plaza gives Kansas City swine diners a second ideally located Masterpiece. At long last, the Plaza location brings authentic American barbecue that meets the strictest federal definition of the product to one of the city's major tourist attractions.

The original K.C. Masterpiece Barbecue & Grill on Metcalf is upscale but not snooty. It has class, accented with brick, brass, polished wood, and carpeting. It also has personality. It's a living mini-museum of things Kansas City. Photos of jazz greats, national and local personalities, and barbecuers from all over the country add friendliness and a sense of community to the ambience of the restaurant. That friendliness and sense of community is reinforced by the K.C. Masterpiece staff, from the front of the house to the back.

K.C. Masterpiece is another of the few Kansas City barbecue restaurants with so much to offer that you have to keep coming back to try it all. The standard barbecue meats such as ribs, beef, chicken, sausage, and pork are smoked to perfection Kansas City–style and slathered with the famous tomato-based, molasses-laced sauce. A chopped pork Carolina-style sandwich topped with coleslaw is perfect when you're in a mood for something different.

If you have a yen for a grilled item, K.C. Masterpiece is the perfect place to get it. Feeling like you have to go light on the calories today? Try one of several grilled chicken breast delicacies. Never had a famous Kansas City strip steak? There's no better place on earth to order your first one and many more to follow than at K.C. Masterpiece.

The chili, the beans, the dirty rice, the fries, the sinfully rich and delicious desserts. The good things to eat at K.C. Masterpiece just never cease. This is another of the few barbecue restaurants in Kansas City that you should put on your "cannot miss" list.

Applause to the Rich Davis family for giving us some of the best barbecue and barbecue sauce in the world!

Keegan's Bar-B-Q
325 E. 135th St.
Martin City, MO 64145
(816) 942-7550

Cash/credit cards. Table service. Sauce bottled for sale.

Tim Keegan gets my vote for being one of the most dedicated and skillful pitmasters in Kansas City. He had big shoes to fill when he took over daily operation of Keegan's from his father, but he's filling them well and doing his dad proud.

Keegan's Bar-B-Q is located in a free-standing building with a big parking lot at the end of 135th Street in the vicinity of several other famous Kansas City dining spots. Keegan's attracts its share of customers and then some. One visit shows you why.

When you step inside Keegan's dining room you could get confused about whether you've entered a storefront gospel house or a barbecue restaurant. The dark simulated wood paneling and mock stained glass window suggest a hint of religiosity. Keegan's isn't a gospel house, but Tim is religious about his mission to smoke the best barbecue in the world for you. When you've seen and tasted Keegan's barbecue, you'll be thankful for Tim's calling.

I've tried everything at Keegan's and never been disappointed. What I return to most often is the burnt ends and the ribs. Both are packed with flavor and smoke that can only get there the old-fashioned way, in Tim's custom-designed pit. A prominent feature is easy-to-chew tenderness. On the side I like Keegan's beans, slaw, and fries.

Keegan's mild sauce is tomato-based, leaning to the sweet side preferred in Kansas City. The hot variety is less sweet, with a tolerable measure of fire. When I mix the two together in equal quantities, the result is fantastic on the meat and with the fries.

The Keegan's staff is some of the friendliest in town. The servers have mastered the art of being friendly and efficient in a very busy setting. Skill and dedication are what it takes to do the job as well as they do it. Tim's example is contagious. So is his barbecue.

Knight's Barbecue
6225 Winner Rd.
Kansas City, MO 64125
(816) 483-7610

Cash. Dine in/carryout/drive through/walk-up.

It takes awhile to get noticed among the scores of barbecue restaurants in Kansas City, but when you're really good, word gets around. That's what's happening at the intersection of Winner Road and Independence Avenue. After getting started only a few years ago, Knight's is fast becoming known as a great place to stop for 'Que.

Knight's is a small place, seating 25 inside and more out on the patio, weather permitting. The light brown simulated wood paneling gives Knight's a friendly feel when you walk in, and that's intended. Knight's is a family enterprise. Betty, James, Jerry, and Karla will treat you like family, too, from the moment you enter. As Betty says, "All of our customers are really close to us. They like us and we like them."

The paneling, the Coca Cola artifacts, and the old-fashioned prints that remind me of my Aunt Mae's cabin in the Ozarks long ago enhance the feeling of friendliness at Knight's. And it's only natural that friendliness is served on the plate also. I mean *really* friendly. The ribs, the brisket, and the chicken are cooked and smoked with 100% hickory logs and tender loving care in a homemade pit. Your taste buds will immediately recognize and welcome the friendly taste. Knight's sauce is friendly, too. Betty calls it an "in between" sauce, "not too hot and not too mild." She's right. The degree of hotness is right in the middle. But when it comes to flavor, Knight's sauce goes beyond middle toward the upper end of excellent. It's the right complement to Knight's barbecue meat.

Knight's hickory-smoked baked beans are outstanding, as is the homemade coleslaw, which has a slight pickle relish accent. Fries, potato salad, onion rings, chili, and chicken chunks round out the side orders menu.

It's against my principles to mention Knight's corn

dogs. But if you must order one, please do it as an act of state fair nostalgia. And by all means slather it with Knight's barbecue sauce.

The motto at Knight's is "Let's Pig Out!" You'll want to do nothing less than that from the first bite to the last. Knight's is on Winner Road for a good reason.

Lil' Jake's Eat It & Beat It
1227 Grand Ave.
Kansas City, MO 64106
(816) 283-0880

Cash. Counter service & carryout. Sauce bottled for sale.

Danny Edwards and his pit crew are single-mindedly serious about one thing and one thing only: preparing and serving good barbecue.

Don't expect fancy surroundings in this downtown hideaway in a parking lot. Don't expect a smile, though smiles aren't unseen on the premises—especially on the faces of satisfied customers. Don't even expect to sit down. A lot of the business here is carryout. If you're fortunate enough to get a seat, Danny means it: Eat it and beat it, so someone else can be seated. It's gotta be that way when there's only 18 seats along four rows of countertops.

I keep coming back to Lil' Jake's for the excellent, tender, smoky beef sandwich with a side order of coleslaw. I've also enjoyed some wonderful chicken wings, a grilled chicken breast sandwich, and Danny's famous Mexican chili (served only in winter months, darn it!). For extra fire to enhance the mildness of Danny's tasty, tomato-based sauce, ask for the shaker of powdered African Bird chili peppers. Sprinkle lightly if you value your tongue.

While dining or waiting for a seat at Lil' Jake's, take note of the memorabilia on the walls. Postcards, barbecue contest ribbons and trophies, and especially the portraits and photos of Danny's legendary K.C. pitmaster father, the late Jake Edwards.

Lil' Jake's Eat It & Beat It is small in size, monumental in taste, and a living Kansas City treasure. Go. Eat. Leave. Go again.

Longbranch Saloon
Seville Square on the Plaza
500 Nichols Rd.
Kansas City, MO 64112
(816) 931-2755

8600 Marshall Dr.
Lenexa, KS 66215
(913) 894-5334

8951 Metcalf Ave.
Overland Park, KS 66212
(913) 642-2042

Cash/credit cards. Table service.

This isn't a greasehouse, and it doesn't pretend to be. It's a saloon that features a few "BBQ" items among a selection of steaks, award-winning hamburgers, salads, deli-style sandwiches, and some Mexican offerings. The "BBQ" is beef, chicken, and pork ribs.

Longbranch servers are touted as "K.C.'s meanest," and the bartenders "can sing, juggle, and talk." In this very popular Kansas City hangout, it's easy to blend into the woodwork and visit, people-watch, and eat. There's lots of woodwork, creating a vision of how the original Longbranch in Dodge City could have looked. On the walls all over the place are tacked notes of wisdom and humor, old product signs, a poster-sized photo reproduction of Mr. Jack Daniel, and assorted other knickknacks.

My favorite "BBQ" at the Longbranch is the baby back ribs. They are tender, tasty, and complemented with a classic Kansas City sauce. These aren't greasehouse ribs; they're saloon ribs, with only a hint of smoke, perhaps from the sauce.

The Longbranch Saloon is a refreshing stop on those occasions when you want something different in an upbeat atmosphere. A word to the wise: Order coleslaw with your ribs. The balance of vinegar, sugar, cabbage, carrots, and poppy seeds is perfect.

Mark & Jerry's Bar-B-Que Buffet
7405 Nieman Rd.
Shawnee, KS 66203
(913) 631-4301

Cash. Buffet/order & pick-up/carryout. Sauce bottled for sale.

Many championship pitmasters dream of opening their own restaurant. Few do it, and even fewer succeed at it. Mark Schroeger and Jerry Young are doing it with success.

Between the two of them, Mark and Jerry have brought home over 200 awards from barbecue cooking contests in 11 different states, including Tennessee and Georgia. Every day now you can find out why barbecue judges like Mark and Jerry's barbecue so much. Bring a big appetite, because this is a big buffet. Sort of like the table at your family reunion on the county fairgrounds, except it's lighter on hodgepodge and heavier on quality.

Most commercial buffets put the cheaper filler foods at the front of the line, hoping you'll put so much on your plate that there's less room for the more expensive foods. Mark and Jerry don't do that. They put their delicious barbecue meats at the front of the line. For one thing, they're proud of it. For another, they know you came here for barbecue and want to make sure that that's what you get the most of. Yes, their beans, coleslaw, and cheese potatoes are good enough to make a complete meal. But you're here for the barbecue, so the side dishes stay on the side, where they belong.

At Mark and Jerry's barbecue buffet you don't have to think a lot about what to order. You can get it all. Ribs, brisket, turkey, sausage, and ham, all of it smoked just right, seasoned just right, and offering the right amount of tenderness. Slather some of Jerry's award-winning sauce on your barbecue, say your prayers, and let the feast begin. You'll be thankful that Mark and Jerry rescued this former pizza restaurant and made it into a plain, white-walled barbecue palace adorned only with the trappings of barbecue royalty.

Marty's Bar-B-Q
2516 N.E. Vivion Rd.
Kansas City, MO 64118
(816) 453-2222

Cash/credit cards. Table service/catering/custom smoking. Sauce bottled for sale.

Marty's Bar-B-Q is in Kansas City's "Northland," only a mile and a half up Antioch Road from the I-35 north Antioch exit. (Turn left on Antioch after exiting.) Marty's white awning and the restaurant logo, complete with flaming hickory logs, comes into sight as you approach Vivion Road.

Whether you enter in the back through the lounge or in the front through the restaurant, the first thing you'll feel is welcome. The people, the surroundings, and the smell of hickory smoke gives anyone who's serious about barbecue the feeling of "I'm going to like it here." And you *will* like it here.

Marty's is fancy by greasehouse standards. There's lots of wood paneling, etched glass, fancy light fixtures, dark green carpeting, and other touches verging on elegance, but not snootiness. Snoutiness is another matter. There's lots of snoutiness in the form of what owner Jean Tamburello calls "pig-a-feti," which is anything having to do with pigs that can be hung on a wall or put on a shelf. Pigs of cloth, pewter, wood, straw, sticks, paint, ink, and other media are all over the place at Marty's. (Pete Tamburello, Jean's husband, is immortalized as a stuffed pig doll wearing an apron with the name "Pete" on it.) And pig-a-feti is in much better taste than is some of the greasehouse graffiti I've seen over the years.

Jean says most of the pig-a-feti comes from friends and customers. Her reputation for liking pork barbecue makes her a pig-a-feti magnet, and Marty's reputation for serving excellent barbecue in a friendly atmosphere is a customer magnet. People from all over Kansas City are attracted to Marty's, and for good reasons.

First among these is the quality of the traditional barbecue. Marty's customers are seeing smoke rings, tasting hickory smoke, and dipping their meat in Marty's special tomato-based, tangy, peppery sauce. The beef brisket, burnt ends, pork spare ribs, baby back ribs, and turkey at Marty's is outstanding. Add to that the grilled chicken breast sandwich, the Italian steak sandwich, and the Italian sausage, and you see why Marty's customers keep coming back. Everything's good, and there's so much to choose from. Marty's even does a twist on the traditional Memphis-style chopped pork sandwich topped with coleslaw. Marty's sandwich is Texas-style chopped beef brisket topped with coleslaw. Sort of like LBJ in an Elvis leisure suit, but not so funny and much more tasteful.

Marty's chicken is delicious. It comes in three versions: wings, Chicken Little (1/2 chicken), and Chicken Big (whole chicken). And Marty's is one of those welcome places where you'll get real turkey breast, formed by Mother Nature instead of an extruder.

True to her taste for foods with an Italian accent, Jean offers an excellent marinated coleslaw with Italian seasonings and an Italian potato salad besides the already-mentioned delicious Italian sausage and Italian steak sandwich.

I'd be remiss not to mention Marty's homemade cheddar soup and made-from-scratch pit beans. The pit bean pintos start out dry. After soaking, rinsing, and cooking, they are pit-smoked in a special sweet-hot sauce.

Finally, another great thing about Marty's is if you order a day or two ahead of time, you can get real, Southern-style, pit-smoked ham. Jean calls it "sweet and smoky ham."

After trying Marty's just once you'll put the Northland on your regular barbecue itinerary.

Original Smoke Bar-B-Que
8611 Hauser (near 87th & Pflumm, behind Pizza Hut)
Lenexa, KS 66215
(913) 888-6262

Cash/credit cards. Table service/carryout/party menu.

Mo knows smoke. So does his cousin, business partner, and head pitmaster, Mehrdad, who learned his pit skills hands-on at one of the best and most successful barbecue restaurants in Kansas City. In its infancy now, Original Smoke is a Kansas City barbecue success story waiting to happen. As more Kansas Citians and tourists discover the ribs, sausage, burnt ends, and chicken wings here, Westchester Square will be known as "the Original Smoke place."

The moderate lighting, carpeting, beige walls, and wooden shelves adorned with jars and other country artifacts give Original Smoke an Americana feel. Together with the framed prints, oak chairs, dark padded booths, burgundy-vinyl print tablecloths, and brick walled kitchen/prep area, these elements give Original Smoke more of a shopping-mall restaurant air instead of a greasehouse look.

Greasehouse purists may want to order carryout, but those who stay will appreciate the friendly service and family atmosphere. The whole family, including Mo's daughter Mahva, works at assuring a pleasant, satisfying que-linary experience that will entice you to come back for more.

I especially like the Original Smoke variety platter, with ribs, chicken, burnt ends, and sausage. The meaty, tender ribs are some of the best in Kansas City. The sausage and burnt ends are exceptional, and the coleslaw is second to none.

Mehrdad uses 100% hickory smoke to flavor his ribs, brisket, pork, and turkey. He applies a slight sprinkling of dry rub to the chicken. The house sauce is smoky, slightly tangy, and flavorful. It doesn't overpower the flavor of the meat.

You'll notice some evidence of a Nolan Ryan fan on the premises of Original Smoke. Ask Mo about it. You may find a willing story swapper as you "eat Mo barbecue."

O'Toole and Sons Ribs
7044 Troost Ave.
Kansas City, MO 64131
(816) 333-0373

Cash/credit cards. Table service.

The big glossy red-and-white sign at the southwest corner of Gregory and Troost will snag your attention. It's one of several tools intended to make this Gaelic greasehouse's motto—"Kansas City's Best Kept Secret"—a thing of the past.

When you step inside O'Toole and Sons, your attention is beckoned with green. The carpeting, the paper place mat menus, the cloth napkins, and the staffers' bow ties and aprons make it emerald-green clear that O'Toole means Irish. In place of an apostrophe between the O and the T of O'Toole, a shamrock does the job.

The atmosphere at O'Toole and Sons is casual and friendly. The food is delicious. The house specialty ribs are hickory smoked, slathered with a flavorful tomato-based mild sauce and garnished with a sliced triangle of fresh pineapple. If you prefer hot sauce, "Son's" sauce is available, but you have to request it. Benjamin O'Toole, the son, developed the hot sauce to stand independent of the house mild sauce. It makes a statement you will remember.

O'Toole and Sons also offers ham, beef, pork, chicken, and shrimp. Of those, my favorite is the beef. Excellent smoke ring and smoke taste.

The side dishes are homemade and delicious—garden salad, Grandma's Potato Salad, Debra's Curry Rice Salad, baked potatoes, and Mary's Baked Beans. Standard French fries are also available.

Porky's Pit Bar-B-Q
4728 Parallel Pkwy.
Kansas City, KS 66104
(913) 287-9688

Cash. Order/pick-up. Sauce bottled for sale.

When Porky's Pit Bar-B-Q opened for business in 1982, it gave a whole new meaning to the name of nearby Mount Hope Cemetery. In addition to hoping to be raised from the grave on Judgment Day, many a barbecue aficionado who has been laid to rest in Mount Hope since 1982 has surely hoped that Porky's is still in business when the roll is called up yonder. The ribs at Porky's are that good.

Situated in a median strip on Parallel Parkway, Porky's sits proudly as a purveyor of quality barbecue in what appears to be a converted drive-in restaurant. After tasting Porky's ribs, you'll be converted, too. Converted to wanting to stop at Porky's for ribs as often as possible. Eating Porky's tender, smoky, fall-off-the-bones pork spareribs slathered with red, spicy sauce reminiscent of Rosedale's is the next best thing to going to heaven. But as long as there's Porky's, heaven can wait!

Earl Quick's Bar-B-Q
1007 Merriam Ln.
Kansas City, KS 66103
(913) 236-7228

Cash. Table service. Sauce bottled for sale.

Earl Quick's Bar-B-Q sits proudly on a curve of Merriam Lane where you can't miss it if you're going east, but you may miss it if you're going west. That's why there's a sign on the north side of the street advertising Earl's rib or burnt ends specials. When you see that sign, put your left turn signal on and proceed with a left when it's safe. When you're going east, it's a simple matter of making a right turn into Earl's parking lot.

Red, white, and blue are the signature colors at Earl's on the outside. The same scheme continues inside, with additions of orange in the main dining area. When you step inside Earl Quick's Bar-B-Q, you'll be in the smaller counter service and carryout side, which leads to the larger, sit-down dining area with tables and booths. There's nothing fancy about Earl Quick's. It's clean and comfortable and the staff is friendly.

Earl Quick himself, after tending a barbecue pit for over 41 years, has turned daily operations and pit tending duties over to his son, Ron. Earl does keep an eye on the place, however. He maintains a quality control presence.

When you sit down to a selection of Earl Quick's barbecue, you'll know by the look, the smell, and the first bite that Earl has put the pit in very able hands. Earl Quick's barbecue ribs, brisket, and burnt ends meet any picky expert's highest standards of appearance, tenderness, and taste. In fact, Earl proudly displays a proclamation from the International Society of Connoisseurs of the Culinary Art of Bar-B-Que, proclaiming the barbecue at Quick's "to be bar-b-que *sans égaler extraordinaire*."

You'll be so absorbed in the quality of the meat that you may forget to try the beans, coleslaw, and fries. But don't forget. They are designed to provide the perfect complement to the meat, and they do. As does the sauce. It has that Rosedale flavor so familiar in several Wyandotte County barbecue restaurants, and that's as it should be, because no other sauce would go better with this meat.

Each time I savor a 100% hickory-smoked, red, tender, smoky rib from Earl Quick's, I experience a moment of prayerful gratitude that a man named Quick chose slow food instead of fast food to make his mark in food-service history.

Ribs 'n Stuff
11423 Hickman Mills Dr.
Kansas City, MO 64134
(816) 763-1225

Cash. Order/pick-up. Sauce available for sale.

Melody Carter's name conjures up the well-known Carter family of gospel and bluegrass music fame. She isn't related, but her barbecue goes well with bluegrass music, and if she keeps doing what she's doing she'll be another famous Carter.

Melody's rib shack got its name from the previous owner, who had hoped to start a Ribs 'n Stuff chain. There's another of his former restaurants under the same name on N.W. Oldham Parkway, also independently owned.

There's nothing fancy about Melody's Ribs 'n Stuff. The brown, unpretentious building may have been somebody's house back in the 1950s. The interior of simulated wood paneling, a few booths and tables, and country music coming through the wall speakers make it clear that what you have here is a rib shack and some other stuff. I came for the ribs, I loved the ribs, and I keep coming back for more. In addition to the range of barbecue—beef, burnt ends, ribs, and ham—you really can get other stuff, the most popular of which is the hot beef with potatoes and gravy. I haven't tried it yet, but it must be as good or better than at any diner in town, because Melody sure sells a lot of it. Same goes for her specially breaded tenderloin sandwich.

With ribs as good as Melody's, I expected her to tell me she learned it from childhood by watching great pitmasters and then perfecting her method by trial and error. Only the latter part is true, though. She didn't know anything about the restaurant business or about the barbecue method of cooking until she bought Ribs 'n Stuff and taught herself. If GM, her former employer, could do as well, Japan would have a trade deficit.

Melody also developed her own sauce. A tasteful balance between sweet and tangy, it's perfect on her ribs. Melody's ribs with a side order of beans and coleslaw is as good as barbecue can get.

What else attracts so many customers to Melody's Ribs 'n Stuff? It's Melody and her friendliness. "I love my customers," she says. "I try to keep the atmosphere very upbeat. Somewhere you'll want to come back and eat. We're small. You get personal service. I try to make everybody feel at home." When you try Ribs 'n Stuff you'll feel you've found a home.

Ricky's Pit Bar-B-Que
5934 Leavenworth Rd.
Kansas City, KS 66104
(913) 334-7000

Cash/credit cards. Table service. Sauce bottled for sale.

Red is the signature color here. Red logo. Red roof. Red tables, booths, chair seats, cloth napkins, sauce, and more.

Barbecue is what you want, and owner/head pitmaster Ricky Smith won't mind if he catches you red-handed with a rib in your mouth and an exclamation in your eyes echoing Ed Asner's endorsement that this is "The Greatest!"

Ricky's ribs are crispy on the outside, tender on the inside. The kiss of hickory smoke, combined with the sweetness from the rub and balanced by the tang in the sauce, will bring a smile to your face. For your side dishes don't miss Ricky's famous pit beans, the homemade coleslaw, and his sweet potato pie.

Rosedale Barbeque
600 Southwest Blvd.
Kansas City, KS 66103
(913) 262-0343

Cash. Order/pick-up on either side of the bar. Sauce bottled for sale.

The parking lot of the original Rosedale's was paved with rib bones. After a busy day the net income was seldom above the price on today's slab of ribs.

At the latest incarnation of the oldest continuously operated barbecue restaurant in Kansas City, the parking lot is paved with asphalt. Prices have kept pace with inflation, but a plate of 'Que at Rosedale's is still one of the best barbecue bargains in America today.

The old red and white "Rosedale Barbecue" sign that served so well for many years was moved to the new parking lot next door to the old place. The new Rosedale's, though bigger, maintains the integrity of the old. The red brick rectangular structure sports brown-tinted windows and wide brown aluminum-slat decorative awnings that hug the building. The dining area is L-shaped and doesn't show the wear of years yet. The linoleum tile floors, stucco and knotty-pine walls, simulated woodgrain Formica-topped tables, and metal-framed chairs with orange-vinyl padding take a step toward the modern while maintaining an echo of the past.

Rosedale ribs and the Rosedale beef sandwich are some of my all-time favorites. Slather your ribs and beef with the famous Rosedale sauce, which has inspired at least a dozen other local sauces. This is one of the "must visit" barbecue institutions of Kansas City.

Rouse's Bar-B-Que
13030 Shawnee Mission Pkwy.
Shawnee, KS 66216
(913) 631-2727

Cash/credit cards. Order/pick-up & drive through. Sauce bottled for sale.

What can you expect when you're driving on busy Shawnee Mission Parkway and you see a barbecue sign with an unusual name that you're not sure how to pronounce?

Rouse's Bar-B-Que in Shawnee is in an out-of-the-way building about a block and a half from the frontage road. The name (pronounced with an "ow" as in "ouch") belongs to Ed Rouse, founder and head pitmaster, who brought his pit skills to Kansas City from North Carolina. Ed does the barbecue at Rouse's. His daughter, Lisa Lawrence, runs the restaurant, with help from mother Lucille Rouse and husband Andy. You'll say "wow!" instead of "ouch" when you eat Rouse barbecue.

This big new sand-colored brick building is freestanding and was built to specifications for Rouse's. Though the outfit doesn't have a long history in Kansas City yet, it has a distinguished one. Rouse's has survived beyond the critical five years in which many restaurants fail. Its sauce has garnered honors in the extremely competitive American Royal International Barbecue Sauce Contest, and it has survived in a location without high visibility. When people find you in an out-of-the-way place and keep coming back, you're doing something right.

Blue is the signature color of Rouse's decor and corporate image, and American country is the style. Modestly frilly curtains, hanging plants, stained woodwork, blue and white paint, carpeted dining area, and acoustical tile ceiling carry out the theme. Rouse's is almost so clean that you might wonder if it could really qualify as a greasehouse and if the barbecue could be any good. The answers to those concerns are, yes, a good greasehouse can be and should be clean, and yes, the barbecue at Rouse's is not only good, it is excellent.

Rouse's various dinner plates are reasonably priced, quite generous, and so satisfying in taste that you'll come back for more. More on another day, that is, as you'll be awfully full when you finish a dinner at Rouse's. One of my favorites here is the variety dinner. It combines ribs, sausage, and burnt ends with Texas toast, a pickle, and a choice of one side dish—coleslaw, potato salad, barbecue beans, French fries, onion rings, tossed salad, or potato chips. Pay extra and get the coleslaw, potato salad, and beans. All three are homemade and delicious.

If you're dining with friends, order several selections from the menu and share. The variety dinner doesn't include Rouse's slow-smoked, lean, tasty beef brisket, which you shouldn't leave without trying. If you're alone, get the combination dinner with ribs, beef, and sausage, or your choice of ham, pork, turkey, or chicken. Just don't omit ribs and beef, as Rouse's does a superior job with both.

Rouse's has a friendly ambience, owing to the management, the staff, and the patrons. You can tell that people feel relaxed and like it here, and most have been here before.

Rouse's Bar-B-Que has put the city of Shawnee on the Kansas City barbecue restaurant map. And although it's back from the main highway a piece, it's easy to find. When you see the Rouse's sign along Shawnee Mission Parkway, expect to find quality barbecue. Ed, Lisa, Lucille, and Andy will make you glad you stopped.

Rustler's Hickory Pit Bar-B-Q
14220 E. 42nd St.
Kansas City, MO 64055
(816) 373-4226

Cash/credit cards. Order/pick-up.

Rustler's Hickory Pit Bar-B-Q stands as a beacon on the hill to those speeding west on I-70 toward the Royals/Chiefs sports complex. It would be wonderful if travelers had direct access to Rustler's from the interstate. Then again, it would surely cause such a traffic tie-up that the highway authorities would soon change back to the present arrangement. And that's all right, because the status quo at Rustler's is very good indeed, and the access isn't difficult. Just exit at Noland Road, go south on 42nd Street to the light, turn left, and follow your nose.

The decor here reflects a cattle rustler theme. Lightly stained knotty-pine walls set a Western mood, especially with the ranch logos branded onto the wood. Prints of scenes from cattle drives add interest, and a "celebrity wall" features famous country-western singers and movie cowpokes who have tried Rustler's Hickory Pit Bar-B-Q and liked it and said so right there with the autograph on their framed photos.

Hanging plants above the divider wall between the serving counter and dining room add a nice touch of green for cowpokes who appreciate something domestic after a rough day on the prairie.

There's lots of room at Rustler's, and it's needed. Thousands of Kansas Citians make regular pit stops here to sit at one of the many tables or booths and relax with tender, smoky ribs, beef, chicken, pork, sausage, or ham. It feeds, sustains, and makes one thankful to be in Kansas City at this place, this time, this feast.

Santa Fe Trail Bar-B-Q
2049 E. Santa Fe
Olathe, KS 66062
(913) 782-7352

Cash/credit cards. Order/pick-up. Sauce bottled for sale.

If Santa Fe Trail Bar-B-Q had actually been on the Santa Fe Trail when settlers passed Olathe on horseback and in covered wagons, the trail would have come to an abrupt stop. Once a pioneer bit into a barbecued rib or a handful of beef, he or she would have traveled no further. The proof is in the phenomenal growth of Olathe since Santa Fe Trail Bar-B-Q first opened.

The original restaurant was closer to downtown, on the west side of I-35. Now it's on the east side of I-35, in the nearby Crossroads Shopping Center. Keeping pace with Olathe's growth, the size of the restaurant has also grown. Big. It's big enough for urban cowpersons to kick off their boots and sit down to some of the finest 'Que a cowperson could ever want. The Western decor, featuring simulated wood paneling, mounted bull horns, and trail roundup prints, is almost swallowed up by the size of the dining area. Your Tony Lamas will stand on carpeted floors and your Stetson will be wafted by gentle breezes from ornamental wood and brass fans descending from the high ceiling. It ain't the prairie, but you ain't no cowpoke.

Santa Fe Trail serves ribs, beef, ham, pork, turkey, sausage, and chicken. For the minority of Olatheans who settled here by accident and have no taste for barbecue, the "H" food is available—hamburgers and hot dogs, not to mention tenderloin sandwiches and chili. Side dishes include coleslaw, beans, potato salad, fries (crinkled or wedged), peppers, and pickles. Cheesecake, cherry pie, and apple pie will feed your sweet tooth.

The best foods in the house are the ribs and the beef. The ribs are smoked all the way to the bone, imparting enough tenderness and flavor to make you wish you could eat the bone. You'll see the smoke ring on the beef and you'll taste the smoke the way it ought to taste—mellow, not bitter. It's almost tender enough for a teething infant. But give baby a clean rib instead. This food is too good to play with.

Santa Fe's tomatoey, spicy sauce has a laid-back Rosedale accent. It doesn't overpower the flavor of the meat, but the meat is good enough to stand alone.

7th Street Bar-B-Q
709 Cheyenne St.
Kansas City, KS 66105
(913) 371-1599

Cash. Table service/carryout (individual and party quantities). Sauce bottled for sale.

After you cross the 7th Street Bridge headed north of the KU Medical Center neighborhood, you'll see the 7th Street Bar-B-Q on Cheyenne Street to your left. It's illegal to turn left from the northbound lane until you've gone a block beyond Cheyenne. You have to turn around and come back, then make a legal right turn on Cheyenne. It's worth the fancy footwork, though. At 7th Street Bar-B-Q you'll find 100% hickory-smoked barbecue, a product of the tender care and expertise of pitmasters Scott and Steve Quick and their pit crew.

The owners used to call this place "Quick's 7th Street Bar-B-Q," but to avoid confusion with the other Quick's barbecue restaurants in town, the new, preferred name is 7th Street Bar-B-Q. Confusion is impossible among the steady patrons, however, as 7th Street Bar-B-Q has been serving quality barbecue at the same location for almost 40 years.

This clean, basic greasehouse is made of cinder blocks painted white and red. Inside is nothing fancy—plain linoleum floors, dark rough wood paneling on the walls, padded-bench booths, Formica-topped tables, textured plastic chairs—sort of a hodgepodge of this and that. It's the kind of greasehouse interior that says the proprietors are more concerned about the quality of the meat than about an orchestrated design. That's how it is and how it should be.

My favorite at 7th Street is the ribs, hands down. These tender, smoky, delicious morsels are about as good as ribs can be. The burnt ends run a close second, though.

When ordering side dishes at 7th Street, don't pass up the coleslaw, potato salad, French fries, or onion rings. Superior Onion Rings does business right next door, so naturally the onion rings here are superior. The same is true of the 7th Street barbecue.

Smoke Stack Bar-B-Q of Martin City
13441 Holmes Rd.
Martin City, MO 64145
(816) 942-9141

Cash/credit cards. Table service. Sauce bottled for sale.

Jack Fiorella's Smoke Stack Bar-B-Q of Martin City is a que-linary complement to the Martin City Melodrama next door. The decor and the menu imitate the days when melodrama first flourished. To paraphrase a remark made by Brenda Brock, a.k.a. Brenda McGillis of ABC-TV's "One Life to Live," about competition 'Que, at Smoke Stack the drama is on the plate.

While following your host through the Smoke Stack dining rooms enroute to your table, you may get the impression that Smoke Stack has grown a room at a time and is still growing. That's a likely hypothesis. Jack's pit crew smokes and serves some of the best barbecue in the world, and judging from the crowds that consistently pour in, the whole world is discovering it.

There is Generic Greasehouse and there is Greasehouse Elegance. Smoke Stack definitely exemplifies the latter. The symphony of wood-paneled walls, Victorian floral print paper, brass fixtures, lamps, ceiling fans, porcelain and porcine artifacts make Smoke Stack elegant but not arrogant. You can eat 'Que here in bib overalls and a gimme cap or tails and a top hat and not look out of place. You will be so absorbed in savoring the food that you won't be concerned about your appearance anyway.

Smoke Stack features barbecue that isn't easy to find in K.C.—beef ribs, baby Denver lamb ribs, and fresh smoked fish. The beef ribs compare favorably to the beef ribs at Oklahoma County Line in Oklahoma City. Lamb aficionados from Moonlite Barbecue in Owensboro, Kentucky, to Kiwi Quisine in New Zealand will not be disappointed with Jack's rack of lamb ribs.

Smoke Stack's pork sausage tastes homemade excellent, the pork spareribs have just the right kiss of smoke and tenderness, and the chicken is outstanding. Burnt ends are popular, but my favorites are pork ribs and lamb ribs. Fish lovers will applaud the offerings here.

If you're dining with someone who doesn't want barbecue, suggest the battered, deep-fried chicken livers. Your vegetarian friends will rave about the Smoke Stack baked potatoes, salad, and onion rings served on a wooden spindle, stacked like a tower.

Smoke Stack side dishes worth cheering about are the salads, fresh coleslaw, onion rings, and pit beans. The latter are incredible, swimming in a thick, saucy bean liquor mixed with pieces of smoked beef and ham. These heavenly legumes are some of the best in Kansas City.

Beer drinkers will find at least one of their favorite brews in the long list of offerings, including Kansas City's own Boulevard Beer on tap.

After partaking of the mellow drama on your plate at Smoke Stack, you'll be ready to relax and cheer and boo in the Martin City Melodrama next door. It will be an entertaining transition from vittles to villains.

Note: There are also two other Smoke Stack establishments to try, one on Wornall Road and one on Highway 71.

Smokin' Joe's BBQ
519 E. Santa Fe
Olathe, KS 66061
(913) 780-5511

Cash. Order/pick-up. Sauce bottled for sale.

Olatheans are just darned lucky. Three excellent barbecue establishments on the east side of the tracks, and one on the other side of the tracks. The latter is Smokin' Joe's. It's the nearest rib house to the seat of Johnson County government and to some of the infamous places described by the late Truman Capote in his tale of *In Cold Blood*. The nearness is purely coincidental, however, because Smokin' Joe's has nothing whatsoever to do with politics or murder. Smokin' Joe's has to do with great barbecue.

Smokin' Joe's BBQ may be Olathe's smallest greasehouse, but the quality of the barbecue is as competitive as the other three. And there's no need to debate which one is best when you can enjoy them all. Let your mood guide you.

When the spirit moves you toward Smokin' Joe's, you'll find it to your left if you're headed west toward the courthouse, to your right if you're headed east away from the courthouse. As with a majority of greasehouses across America, Smokin' Joe's looks like a convert from something else, maybe a fast food taco place. It doesn't matter. Smokin' Joe's was sufficiently renovated to give it the character of an authentic barbecue restaurant both outside and in.

Inside, Smokin' Joe's is decorated with antique artifacts from Midwestern farm life, plus photos of horses and horse breeders, Andy Devine, and miscellaneous subjects of the type you might find in a big trunk in Grandma's attic.

Thousands of people with life's milestone events on their minds pass Smokin' Joe's every weekday. No other greasehouse in Johnson County can lay claim to that. Marriage, adoption, divorce, crime, court settlements, they all pass Smokin' Joe's. The challenge is how to get them to stop. Smokin' Joe does it with smoke. When the smoke hits the nostrils, it sends a message to the tummy, setting off a jump start in the brain, and they stop.

My favorites at Smokin' Joe's are the ribs, with beans, fries, and slaw on the side. These ribs are smoked to perfection the old-fashioned way, covered with award-winning sauce. What better way to celebrate or mourn another of life's milestones. You'll be glad Smokin' Joe got your attention.

Snead's Corner Bar-B-Q
801 E. 171st St. (171st & Holmes Rd.)
Belton, MO 64012
(816) 331-9858

Cash/credit cards. Table service. Sauce bottled for sale.

When the friendly aproned mothers and daughters of rural Missouri put your platter of 'Que on the table at Snead's, you'll know it was worth the drive. The hickory-smoked selection of meats here is fresh, tender, and delicious. Turkey, ham, pork, beef, burnt ends—called "brownies" of beef or ham at Snead's—and ribs have attracted tens of thousands of hungry customers to this hilltop barbecue beacon for almost four decades.

Snead's isn't as far into the country now as it was when the original owner, Bill Snead, first opened it, but you'll still feel like you're taking a mini rural expedition as you drive there. When you step inside, the feeling continues. The original main dining room, with its dark wood panels, mounted deer heads, hanging plastic plants, and other touches that your country grandmother would have added, give Snead's a warm, comfortable ambience. This feeling also pervades the second dining room, with windows that showcase the countryside, and the new dining room as well, which expanded Snead's capacity to 200.

The diners in all three rooms often behave as if everyone is there for a big family reunion. The friendly staff and management encourage this atmosphere. They even bring each guest a free ice cream cone at the end of the meal.

Many Snead's regulars swear by the brownies. For me, the ribs top the list. Snead's homemade beans and coleslaw provide the perfect balance, along with the Suzy Q curly fried potatoes. A bite of rib, a bite from each side dish, chased with a sip of cold brew from a frosty mug, and you'll understand why Alan Richman, a writer for *People* magazine, put Snead's in America's Top 10 barbecue restaurants.

Werner's Specialty Foods
5736 Johnson Dr.
Mission, KS 66202
(913) 362-5955

Cash. Ribs, brats, franks, & Italian sausages to go. Sauce negotiable.

It's not often that I'll settle for baked and sauced baby back ribs, but the way Werner does them makes me violate my principles. The quality of these ribs has everything to do with Werner himself, first and foremost a man who knows meat and insists on the best. That's another reason I've put him in this book, for the benefit of competition pitmasters looking for an edge.

Before moving to America, Werner was trained as a skilled butcher in his native Germany. Upon arrival in the United States, he learned the American way with meat, from packing house to point-of-purchase. Before venturing into business on his own, he worked at Swanson's in Westport, where he added some Swedish and Norwegian ways to his repertoire. Today, people drive all the way from Topeka and further for Werner's Norwegian potato sausage.

Werner doesn't use fire and smoke to cook his baby back ribs, but those that come from his oven, slathered with his own special sauce, can just about fool the experts. The meat is lean, tender, and flavorful. It almost melts in your mouth.

On Saturdays, weather permitting, Werner's staffers fire up the charcoal in a large cooker and grill three varieties of Werner's famous sausage for sale in a bun. Instead of deciding between a bratwurst, frankfurter, or Italian sausage, get all three. Or, do as I do, and get a different one each time you're lucky enough to be at Werner's when the grill is fired up and the franks and sausages aren't sold out. Standard condiments are German mustard and catsup, but if you ask grillmaster Steve Bruner to see if he can negotiate some sauce from Werner for you, and if he does so successfully, you just may be treating yourself to the best grilled bratwurst in the universe.

While you're in Werner's neighborhood, check out nearby Corky's Records and Tapes. Corky knows music, including the stuff that goes well with barbecue.

Another required stop in Werner's neighborhood is Hartman and Sons Hardware. Here you can buy the best blend of chili spices in America. After trying Hartman's Chili Powder you'll never again settle for anything less. It's all waiting for you on a refreshing little stretch of Johnson Drive.

Westport Bar-B-Que
4181 Broadway
Kansas City, MO 64111
(816) 931-3235

11308 Blue Ridge Blvd.
Kansas City, MO 64134
(816) 763-0085

Cash. Order/pick-up.

The Battle of Westport wouldn't have happened if John and Rosie Grant had been on the scene. Hickory smoke from Grant's Pit would have lured Union and Confederate soldiers to eat barbecue instead of do battle.

But John and Rosie's appointment with history came later. The Civil War raged on and others followed. The one in Vietnam is memorialized right across the street from Westport Bar-B-Que.

Westport Bar-B-Que exemplifies the Greasehouse Eclectic style of decor. The walls are adorned with decoupaged ads, currency, and announcements from the Civil War era, plus assorted artifacts, dime store French Impressionist reproductions, and beer signs. One entire wall is stainless steel. The floor is black and white–checkered linoleum, bistro-style. Tables are brown and square; two are like the ones in Wendy's, with old-fashioned catalog ads in the Formica.

Although John's other career was in the hamburger industry, his hickory-smoked pork spare ribs bear no resemblance to the boneless, extruder-molded variety so popular with those who eat in the fast food lane. These ribs are real, with a smoky flavor that pairs well with John and Rosie's secret sauce. The tomato-based sweetness of the sauce follows the Kansas City tradition; a balanced blend of spices give it the Grants' special signature.

Don't pass up the beef brisket, either. It's very lean, with a perfect smoke ring and just the right kiss of smoke. Dieters will like the popular Westport Bar-B-Que chicken breast.

Side dish choices are homemade and delicious—especially the beans, coleslaw, and pasta salad.

Plaza area business persons, neighbors, and tourists are spreading the word and 'Queing up at Westport Bar-B-Que. Same goes for people in southeast Kansas City at Westport's Blue Ridge Boulevard location.

After lunch at Westport Bar-B-Que, visit the Vietnam Memorial, then go a few blocks west to Wornall and south to Jacob Loose Park, scene of the Battle of Westport. Reflect upon history and stop to smell the roses.

Winslow's City Market Smokehouse
20 E. Fifth St.
Kansas City, MO 64106
(816) 471-RIBS

Cash/credit cards. Order/pick-up. Sauce bottled for sale.

Barbecue belongs in City Market. Here, where the tradition of bartering and selling fish, fowl, and produce fresh from the streams, barnyards, and gardens of the Heartland is still alive and thriving, it's fitting that buyers and sellers have a great place to eat barbecue together, at Winslow's City Market Smokehouse.

A step inside Winslow's is like a step into the smokehouse past of the 1950s. Although the entire restaurant is newly remodeled, it maintains the feel of mid-20th century America. The brick, wood, picnic tables, benches, and ceramic tile floors feel warm, welcome, and familiar.

The usual variety of barbecue is sold at Winslow's—ribs, beef, chicken, pork, and turkey. Familiar side dishes such as fries, coleslaw, and beans also are available. My favorite for taste and value is the beef sandwich. The beef is lean, with a beautiful smoke ring and just the right touch of smoke.

Winslow's sauce perfectly complements their meat. I expected the black strap molasses in the sauce to impart the signature taste, but to me it's the vinegar, laced with spices and tomato, that signs the name "Winslow" on this sauce. It's pricey by the bottle, but worth it. Squeeze bottles of it sit on the tables for liberal use while dining at Winslow's.

Don Winslow, head pitmaster, and his mother Addie have been partners in the City Market Smokehouse since 1972. Together they've made a barbecue tradition come alive and thrive in Kansas City's "Pioneer Central."

Wyandot Bar-B-Q
8441 State Ave.
Kansas City, KS 66112
(913) 788-7554

7215 W. 75th St.
Overland Park, KS 66204
(913) 341-0609

Cash. Order/pick-up. Sauce bottled for sale.

From the outside, Wyandot No. 1 on State Avenue looks like a weathered little barbecue shack you'd expect to find nestled among the hills. When you step inside, you're surrounded by real, rough-cut weathered wooden walls, and you think, "Maybe this is the Ozarks."

The photos of Dobermans and the hunting trophies—stag, antelope, wild boar—may suggest to you that redneck is spoken here. It is. Owner/head pitmaster Ron Williams may not smile at you, but he won't growl at you either. What he'll do is serve you a slab of ribs or a beef sandwich worth writing to Mama about. Disregard the absence of smoke rings. Wyandot barbecue tastes smoked and is smoked, but the smoke rings are often faded out. It still tastes great. Ron's sauce has a Rosedale accent, with or without hotness.

The food reaches the same excellence at No. 2, served in a suburban fast food setting.

Zarda Bar-B-Q
11931 W. 87th St.
Lenexa, KS 66215
(913) 492-2330

214 N. 7 Hwy.
Blue Springs, MO 64015
(816) 229-9999

Cash/credit cards. Order/pick-up & drive through. Sauce bottled for sale throughout the metropolitan area.

Zarda Bar-B-Q, at the sign of the pig in flames wafting a frosty, foamy beer mug, needs no introduction to Kansas Citians. Zarda belongs at the end of the Kansas City barbecue alphabet because for thousands of loyal customers it's the last word.

On the outside, the Zarda brothers—Steve and Mike—leave no doubt that their establishment uses hickory for smoke and fire. It's stacked right out front where you can see it. Their free-standing building of brick and wood, roofed with wooden shingles, is better than a red carpet for the hungry masses of "Sowtown Central."

Zarda is big inside. It has to be to accommodate so many customers. The design of the interior, however, hides the magnitude of the space with the creation of several dining areas. The decor, too, adds a warmth that cuts Zarda down to a friendly size. Real wood walls, mounted longhorns, and lighting that's neither too bright nor too dim enhance the overall ambience.

My Zarda favorites are the beef and pork combo sandwich, the burnt ends, and the ribs. Throw in Zarda's excellent beans and an order of onion rings, a bottle of Zarda's classic Kansas City sauce, and let's not talk until our plates are clean.

KANSAS CITY BARBECUE GIFTS AND PRODUCTS

Leaving Kansas City without barbecue is as unthinkable as leaving Vermont without maple syrup. Fortunately, it's easy to find the right product for your needs. If your bags are too overloaded for a slab of ribs, there's always room for a rib rub in your purse or pocket and a bottle of sauce in your briefcase. You can also purchase products for carrier delivery to your door and the doors of friends and relatives who expect you to remember them.

With advance notice most Kansas City barbecue restaurants will freeze a slab of ribs and package them for your trip home. Frozen ribs travel well for several hours. When zapped in a microwave, they taste just like they're fresh from the pit.

If you can't carry ribs, take sauce. You mustn't leave Kansas City without barbecue sauce. Sauces are available from many of the restaurants featured in this book and all of the stores featured in this section.

Rib rubs are especially fun to give for birthdays, anniversaries, Valentine's Day, and other special occasions. You'll be thanked and remembered.

A T-shirt from Boardroom, Rosedale's, or any other K.C. BBQ restaurant is always appropriate. Another winner is the Charlie Podrebarac classic series of Cowtown barbecue T-shirts. His "Night of the Living Barbecue" is loved by hardcore pitmasters *and* vegetarian activists.

Take a minute to make up your gift list and pick a store or two from this guide. The rest is easy and fun.

The Best of Kansas City
6233 Brookside Plaza
Kansas City, MO 64113
(816) 333-7900

Crown Center
2450 Grand Ave.
Kansas City, MO 64108
(816) 842-0200

The Best of Kansas City opened its first retail store in the Brookside area in 1982 and has been featuring fine products made in Kansas City ever since. Owner Karen Nash keeps plenty of barbecue items on hand, from sauces and seasonings to books, aprons, and grilling gift packs. Items may be purchased separately or grouped appealingly into bountiful barbecue baskets. The basket trade is a signature of these shops, but one of the most popular gift items is the Best of Kansas City Barbeque Three Pack, which includes Gates, Bodee's, and Hayward's sauces. Kansas City is lauded for its fine beef, and Best of Kansas City also ships USDA bacon-wrapped filets and Kansas City strip steaks guaranteed throughout the United States.

In 1986 Karen opened her second shop in the tony Crown Center Shops and found her niche with a unique selection of gifts from Kansas City. As always, the most popular barbecue items find themselves traveling all over the world. Call (800) 366-8780 for a catalog complete with photos and descriptions of the basket offerings.

Catch Kansas City
The Plaza
608 W. 48th St.
Kansas City, MO 64112
(816) 753-7221

Allis Plaza Hotel
200 W. 12th St.
Kansas City, MO 64105
(816) 421-6800, ext. 4474

Oak Park Mall
95th St. & Quivira Rd.
Overland Park, KS 66214
(913) 888-2260

Walking into these stores is a trendy treat. Each location has its own flair, from the neon lights and black-and-white cow-spotted counters at Oak Park Mall to the high-tech black grid displays at the Plaza store. Cow and pig string lights decorate at Christmas time and all year round. Steer horns adorn the doorways and barbecue reigns supreme. The Catch Kansas City Barbecue Sauce box lets the customer choose three sauces from among Bodee's, Hayward's, Arthur Bryant's, Gates, Flower of the Flames, Jazzy, and Amazing Grace. Catch Kansas City also specializes in a full range of Kansas City souvenirs—T-shirts, caps, mugs, books, prints, and much more.

Halls Crown Center
200 E. 25th St.
Kansas City, MO 64108
(816) 274-8168

Halls Plaza
211 Nichols Rd.
Kansas City, MO 64112
(816) 274-3468

Halls stores are owned by parent company Hallmark Cards, Inc., whose slogan "When you care enough to send the very best" works with the Halls barbecue offerings as well. Here you can get the Cadillac of barbecue rigs, the Hasty Bake Oven, which features a movable grill grid and temperature gauge, a separate fire door, and a drawer easy enough for a novice to operate. Halls also privately labels their own line of barbecue products: Halls Barbeque Seasoning & Rub, Halls Barbeque Salsa, and Halls Barbeque Sauce. Fun summer tableware is a specialty here, and you'll find sublime displays that will have you buying up the store. Don't forget the recipe books and tongs, and you're all set for great Kansas City BBQ.

Kansas Sampler
9548 Antioch Rd.
Overland Park, KS 66212
(913) 383-2920

Don't let the name deceive you—there's plenty here from Missouri, too! Owner/founder Peg Leibert is a vocal advocate of Kansas and Missouri products. She travels both states expounding the historical and gourmet offerings that are part of our heritage. At Kansas Sampler you'll find wheat weavings, sunflower plates, corn husk dolls, handmade pottery, and hand-blown glass, all locally made. There's a fun assortment of T-shirts as well as a book lovers' nook, complete with historicals on the Wild Wild West, flora and fauna of the two states, guidebooks, cookbooks, and barbecue books. Peg stocks lots and lots of gourmet items—jams, honeys, herb-flavored vinegars, and bakery mixes—and lots and lots of BBQ items—sauces, spices and rubs, books, aprons, relishes, woods, and smoker kits. All may be purchased individually or gathered to make your own Kansas or Missouri sampler box, mailable to wherever your heart desires.

Lotta Hotta
Oak Park Mall
11721 W. 95th St.
Overland Park, KS 66214
(913) 599-0023

Ward Parkway Shopping Center
8600 Ward Pkwy.
Kansas City, MO 64114
(816) 333-5177

Bannister Mall
5600 Bannister Rd.
Kansas City, MO 64137
(816) 765-2743

Wow! If you like HOT, you've found home at Lotta Hotta. Here's Kansas City's best and biggest array of hot stuff under one roof. The hot barbecue sauce selection includes a favorite of Kansas Citians, the "Hottest Barbecue Sauce on the Planet," Inner Beauty Real Hot. Read the label: This isn't kid stuff. One local hot barbecue sauce, Vinnie's Soul Sauce (Lotta Hotta's own private label), will put fire in your mouth. Chase it with some Ass Kickin' Peanuts, and you're as hot as the Fourth of July. A full selection of chili powders, T-shirts, spices, chips, condiments, relishes, piñatas, books, and more is sold. Call (800) LOTT-HOT for a free catalog.

Missouri Memories
Seville Square on the Plaza
500 Nichols Rd.
Kansas City, MO 64112
(816) 931-9174

Owner Nancy Welchon founded Missouri Memories in 1984. Located in the Country Club Plaza, this is a "must see" shop to find unique souvenirs from the Show-Me State. A special Mary Engelbreit corner features T-shirts, gift tins, posters, music boxes, and baby items from this nationally recognized St. Louis artist. Appealing animal memorabilia include cats, cows, pigs, dogs, dinos, bears, and frogs, on mugs, greeting cards, stationery, T-shirts, Post-It Notes, and rubber stamps. One of the hottest items here is the "Air Toto" T-shirt, depicting the famous Wizard of Oz canine in red-hot tennis shoes making a Michael Jordan dunk shot. Fun trinkets to take home from this shop include movie buttons, sipper straws, and your very own Kansas twister in a snow dome.

Missouri Memories carries a full line of Missouri and Kansas City books, with several on the topic of barbecue. Kansas City barbecue seasonings include Rick's Rib Rub, BBQ & Grill Seasoning, Kansas City Steak Seasoning and Marinade, and Lemon Butter. Barbecue sauces include Jazzy, Arthur Bryant's, Adrien's, Gates, Hayward's, and Bodee's. A special pack of three barbecue sauces makes an easy take-home gift.

Professional Chef
Crown Center
2450 Grand Ave., Suite 1
Kansas City, MO 64108
(816) 426-1175

Boasting over 60 varieties of predominantly Kansas City barbecue sauce, Professional Chef offers tastings daily. Their own Heartland Bar-B-Que Sauce is available alone or in the Heartland Market Three Pack, along with Gates and Flower of the Flames sauces. Kansas City barbecue is king at this shop, which displays grilling and barbecue books, clever cow aprons, sauces, spices, grill racks, stove-top smokers, heat resistant mitts, flavored wood chips (mesquite, hickory, apple, and cherry)—everything but the grill! This is the place to load up your shopping bag. Custom-made gift baskets are also available. In addition to barbecue, Pro Chef offers top of the line culinary equipment and gourmet gifts. After you stock up, go next door for great barbecue at Heartland Bar-B-Que—they're owned by the same folks!

Pryde's Old Westport
115 Westport Rd.
Kansas City, MO 64111
(816) 531-5588

Pryde's is a treasure trove of gourmet foods, gadgets, tabletop items, wooden chopping blocks, and more. Just about all of your kitchen, dining room, and bar service can be purchased here, all housed in a charming two-story building in "Old Westport." Pryde's barbecue fare is first rate. Over a dozen BBQ sauces are available, and the accessories take the cake. They have baskets for fish, chicken, or hamburgers, different sized grill toppers, temperature gauges, skewers, mitts, aprons, picnic baskets, checkered tablecloths, tongs, spatulas, and numerous long-handled basting brushes and mops. Check out the cookbook nook, which includes barbecue and grill books. Just like the Country Club Plaza, Pryde's is a "must do"!

KANSAS CITY AREA BARBECUE COOKING CONTESTS

One of the best ways to get into the spirit of Kansas City barbecue is to go to a local barbecue cooking contest. You'll get a first-hand look at how seriously barbecuers take their cooking and their fun. You can look, smell, and taste. If you ask when the team isn't busy preparing an entry for the judges, you can get some practical tips on how to improve your own barbecue cooking skills. Advice abounds, though it isn't always consistent. But that way you can choose what sounds best to you.

The following listings are based upon the most accurate information available at the time of publication. Actual cookoff dates may vary from year to year, so it's a good idea to check the local newspapers, contact the Kansas City Barbeque Society (address at the end of this section), or call the contest organizers to make sure of dates, times, and locations.

Each cookoff listed below is sanctioned by the Kansas City Barbeque Society. This means that the contest adheres strictly to the rules, regulations, and judging standards of the Society, and that a representative of the Society is present to assure compliance. A key characteristic of KCBS rules is the requirement that judges not know the identity of the team entries. Each entry is assigned a number known only to contest officials.

APRIL (last Saturday)
KCBS Spring Training Cookoff
This members-only spring ritual of the Kansas City Barbeque Society has attracted the faithful and the hopeful to Dan Haake's farm in Bucyrus, Kansas, since 1985.

MAY (second Saturday)
Blue Devil Cookoff
Wyandotte County Fairgrounds
Kansas City, KS
(913) 334-1100, ext. 132
Begun in 1986 as a benefit for the Kansas City, Kansas, Community College, this is the premier barbecue cooking contest of the season in Wyandotte County.

MAY (last Saturday)
Raytown BBQ Contest
9715 E. 63rd St.
Raytown, MO
(816) 356-0505

The judges occupy the horse barn, the contestants are put out to pasture, and the spectators get maximum exposure to local talent on stage and que-linary talent all over the place. Clowns, horses, music, fun, and food.

JUNE (last Saturday)
Great Lenexa Barbeque Battle
Sar-Ko-Par Park, West 87th St.
Lenexa, KS
(913) 541-8592

The Lenexa battle is the official Kansas state championship and one of the don't-miss barbecue events of the season. One hundred sixty cooking teams compete amidst lots of enthusiastic spectators and lots of fun—and samples of barbecue at its best.

JULY (third Saturday)
Midwest Regional Championship
Public park near the water tower
Gladstone, MO
(816) 436-6126 or (913) 621-5115

The Gladstone organizers of this event go all out to make it fun for spectators and worthwhile for competitors. There's a huge arts and crafts fair tent, vendors of all variety, information booths, and a tent where you can evaluate sauces created by the contestants for the "Iddy-Biddy-Diddy-Wa-Diddy Barbecue Sauce Contest."

AUGUST (first Saturday)
North Kansas City Championship Barbecue Contest
Downtown Kansas City North
(816) 471-4895

A unique feature of this contest is the junior pitmasters competition for children up to age 12. The organizers see to it that cooks of all ages and the spectating public enjoy some inimitable Northland hospitality.

AUGUST (second Saturday)
Great Show-Me State Championship
River Front Park
St. Joseph, MO
(816) 232-0746

This one happens at the riverside in St. Joseph, giving it a magic that can only happen next to rolling waters. Show me to this one and I'll show you some unforgettable barbecue.

SEPTEMBER (second Saturday)
Blue Springs Blaze-Off State Championship
Municipal Park
Blue Springs, MO
(816) 224-3264 or (816) 228-0137

From a small contest near the civic swimming pool, the Blue Springs Barbeque Blaze-Off has grown to major contest status in a few short years. It is well organized and designed to attend to the comfort and entertainment of competitors and spectators alike. Deejay music, retail vendors, and an atmosphere that encourages interaction between competitors and the public are some of the favorite features of the Blaze-Off.

SEPTEMBER (third Saturday)
Jesse James Barbecue Contest
Within sight of the I-35 Exit
Kearney, MO
(816) 635-4229

It's debatable whether "slow and low" is compatible with the lifestyle of the late outlaw Jesse James. There's no debate, however, about the compatibility of the Jesse James Barbecue Contest with Kearney's annual observance of Jesse James Days. Tourists are welcome to share in the nostalgia and in the que-linary products. If you happen to be a Howard, change your name to Jones, Smith, Davis, or Bubba while mingling at the contest.

SEPTEMBER (third Saturday)
Bates County Beef-A-Thon
Bates County Fairgrounds
Butler, MO
(816) 679-3124

Though a relative newcomer, this is already one of the most-favored contests of the competitive pitmasters. The Bates County Beef Council backs this contest with the capital and attention to detail that gets the attention of barbecuers and the barbecue-consuming public and makes everyone glad about participating.

OCTOBER [first Friday & Saturday]
American Royal Barbecue Contests
American Royal Complex
Kansas City, MO
(816) 221-9800

This is another contest of which legends are made. It's big, one of the biggest in the world. And it's fun, because there's so much going on in addition to barbecue. And it's where most of Kansas City can be found on the first Saturday of October.

Contest cooking begins on Thursday night in preparation for the prestigious American Royal International Invitational Barbecue Cooking Contest. The judging on Friday, conducted by panels of internationally recognized experts, is based on how barbecue should look, smell, and taste. Competitors are invited only if they have won a major qualifying barbecue cooking contest.

Saturday is the contest biggie. The main event is the open barbecue cooking contest, with over 200 teams competing for honors. It requires a football field–sized area inside the Governor's Building to accommodate all of the judges.

Another major event on Saturday is the American Royal International Barbecue Sauce Contest. Begun in 1984 as the "Diddy-Wa-Diddy National Barbecue Sauce Contest," it quickly outgrew the founder's patio and has called the American Royal "home" since 1987. It is open to commercially available sauces only. Judges representing a microcosm of the barbecue-consuming public determine the "Best Barbecue Sauce on the Planet" each year from hundreds of entries. Sauces are judged blind;

ballots are computed by a dedicated team of Price Waterhouse volunteers.

Cooking contests featuring ham, chicken wings, and side dishes also take place on Saturday.

A Wild West Show, kiddie rides, barbecue vendors, plus musical and dance entertainment contribute to the popularity of this last barbecue celebration of the season in Kansas City.

And DON'T forget the Diddy-Wa-Diddy Barbecue Store. Barbecue vendors from all over the world donate sauce and other barbecue-related products for sale at the store. Hundreds of Kansas Citians do their annual holiday and special event gift shopping at the Diddy-Wa-Diddy store each October. Buy some championship barbecue at the Kansas City Barbeque Society booth and then try it with free samples of barbecue sauce at the Diddy-Wa-Diddy store.

Proceeds from the American Royal Barbecue benefit the education programs of the American Royal, Kansas City's Chapter of The Dream Factory, the Mid-America Council on Aging Meals for the Homebound Elderly Program, and the Hospitality Management programs at Penn Valley and Johnson County Community Colleges.

Get Connected

People who love barbecue should get together and share information and celebrate and spread the good word that barbecue isn't just for breakfast anymore. They've done it, and you can join them by applying for membership in the Kansas City Barbeque Society. Just send a check made out to KCBS for $15.00 to:

Gary Wells, Ph.B., President
Kansas City Barbeque Society
11514 Hickman Mills Dr.
Kansas City, MO 64134

Gary will send you an application. Once accepted, your check will be processed and you're in. Members keep up-to-date on what's happening through the KCBS *Bullsheet* and cookoff announcements from all over the country.

Amazing Grace's BBQ
#1 Sauce in America!
(1989 American Royal National BBQ Sauce Contest)

Buy Any Food Item and Get One FREE

**Use This Coupon with our Compliments
Grand Emporium
3832 Main 531-7557
Eat In/Carry Out 11AM-11PM**

Buy one sandwich get one Sandwich of equal or lesser value FREE!

Offer good Tuesday and Wednesday for DINE-IN ONLY!

B.B.'s—the home of Bar-B-Q, Blues & Beer.

Our waitresses accept tips.

Crown Center Shops

Brookside Plaza

FREE Best of Kansas City Steak Spice Card with purchase.

Spices included in card are steak baste, steak seasoning, and lemon butter.

Sure to have you grilling better than the guy next door!

BOARDROOM BAR·B·Q

Our Meat is SERIOUS BUSINESS
9600 Antioch
Overland Park, KS 66212

$5.00 off any 2 Combination Platters

SAVE $5.00

$5.00 Off

DINNER FOR 2
With purchase of 2 Dinner Plates!

Not including LITE BITES
Not Valid With Any Other Offer

CATCH KANSAS CITY

10% off our large selection of Kansas City BBQ packs, sauces, spices, and books.
Make Catch Kansas City your BBQ SHOP!

Country Club Plaza	Oak Park Mall	Allis Plaza Hotel
608 W. 48th St.	95th & Quivera	200 W. 12th St.
753-7221	888-2260	421-6800 x 4474

1007 MERRIAM LANE
KANSAS CITY, KS 66103

FREE bottle of Earl Quick's FAMOUS Bar-B-Q Sauce
with any Rib purchase!

FREE sauce offer good any day but Wednesday.

Wednesday is Earl's FAMOUS $8.00 Slab Special!

Our Customers send our ribs nationwide!

$ ONE BUCK OFF
GATES BAR-B-Q
THREE (GIFT) PACK

Redeem at any Gates Bar-B-Q Restaurant

HEARTLAND BARBECUE
Crown Center Shops

Buy one entree and
get the second entree at half-price

HILLSDALE BANK BAR-B-Q

Open Thur., Fri., Sat. & Sun. 11:00-8:00 • phone: 783-4333

Choice of any beef, pork, ham, turkey, or sausage sandwich—

Buy one get one FREE!

Greg & Donna Beverlin — Proprietors

"You Can Bank On Our Ribs!"

KANSAS SAMPLER STORE
9548 ANTIOCH, OVERLAND PARK KS 66212

Worth $1.00 on $10.00 or more purchase of BBQ products.

383-2920
- Gourmet Kansas Foods
- Kansas T-Shirts • Kansas Artists
- Kansas Books • OZ
- Regional College Gifts

Hours:
Mon-Fri: 10-8
Sat: 10-6 & Sun: 1-5

KNIGHTS B-B-Q
DINE IN or CARRY OUT!

INDEP. AVE & WINNER RD.
483-7610
Phone Orders
Walk up Window

$1.00 off one one slab of ribs!
Offer good for dine in or carry out.

10% off Purchase of BBQ Products

Mail Order
Call for Catalog
1-800-LOTT-HOT

3 Locations
Bannister Mall
Oak Park Mall
Ward Parkway Mall

Marty's Bar-B-Q
2516 N. E. Vivion Road
816-453-2222

$1.00 off the purchase of one regular priced sandwich or sandwich plate
OR
$2.00 off the purchase of one regular priced dinner

Offer not good for specials or with the use of other coupons.
DINE IN ONLY

MOO of EVERYTHING

$1 OFF BBQ 3-PACK

MOO T-SHIRTS • MOO TOYS
MOO SOUVENIRS • MOO CARDS
MOO BBQ GIFTS

MOO-SOURI MEMORIES
SEVILLE ON THE PLAZA • LEVEL 2
500 NICHOLS ROAD, KCMO 64112
816-931-9174

O'Toole and Sons RIBS

"Kansas City's Best Kept Secret"

All our meats are slow cooked in Hickory Smoke

Gregory and Troost Ave.
Call for information on Event or Party Catering
333-0373 or 421-7631

$1.00 OFF ANY FOOD ORDER

 PIG OUT PUBLICATIONS, INC.

The Kansas City BBQ Pocket Guide • Passion of Barbeque
Hooked on Fish on the Grill • Barbecue Greats Memphis Style
Bar-B-Que, Barbecue, Barbeque, Bar-B-Q, B-B-Q

FREE Shipping on any BBQ Book(s) ordered from Pig Out Publications!

Mail in coupon with order form at back of book!

Professional Chef
Crown Center Shops

10% off on any BBQ related product

The most extensive BBQ sauce selection in the city!

Rouse's
Bar-B-Que

13030 Shawnee Mission Pkwy., Shawnee, KS 66216. 631-2727

10% off Lunch or Dinner
Offer good Monday through Friday for Dine-in only

- Cocktail Lounge
- Banquet Facility
- Catering
- Daily Specials

Hours:
Mon.-Sat. 11-10 pm
Sun. 11-9 pm

"Best Ribs in K.C."

Smokin' Joe's BBQ

519 E. Santa Fe
Olathe, KS 66061

Buy one dinner get one dinner FREE
Dine in or Carry Out

- Catering
- Carry out
- Smokin' Joe's BBQ Sauce
- Award-winning Hot Sauce

SPECIAL OFFER
Slab for Two with
Two Side Orders
$14.50

(3 1/2 pound slab of ribs is slow-smoked over green hickory wood in Winslow's old style brick barbecue pit.)

Pig Out Publications, Inc. Order Form

Order direct—Call 816-531-3119

Please send me:

_____ copy(s) **Kansas City BBQ Pocket Guide for $7.95**

_____ copy(s) **Barbecue Greats Memphis Style for $12.95**

_____ copy(s) **The Passion of Barbeque for $9.95**

_____ copy(s) **Hooked on Fish on the Grill for $8.95**

_____ copy(s) **Bar-B-Que, Barbecue, Barbeque, Bar-B-Q, B-B-Q for $5.95**

Add $2.00 for Shipping for Each Book Ordered

Method of Payment

____ Enclosed is my check for $ _____ (payable to PIG OUT PUBLICATIONS, INC.)

Please charge to my credit card: _____VISA ____ MasterCard

Acct. #_____ Exp. Date

Signature_____

Ship to: **Gift/Ship to:**

_____   _____

_____   _____

_____   _____

_____   _____

_____   From _____

Mail completed order form to:

Pig Out Publications, Inc. • 4245 Walnut • Kansas City, MO 64111-1718

SWINE DINING FINDS

SWINE DINING FINDS